"Liz Lev gives the best, most rousing, comprehensive, and historically grounded art tours in Rome, and now she shows her gift for bringing art to life in this magnificent new book. In it she casts her knowing, appreciative eye on the beautiful works of Catholic Restoration art, showing how even in the most difficult times, beauty and faith, aligned and entwined, can move mountains. A treat for the eye and the soul."

—Peggy Noonan
Columnist, *Wall Street Journal*

"Liz Lev so brilliantly connects art and faith that you will experience every painting, statue, and church in a deeper, emotionally powerful, and spiritually fulfilling way. A beautiful, breathtaking achievement in a beautiful book."

—Newt Gingrich

"Many talk today about evangelization through beauty. In a series of finely crafted and absorbing essays, Elizabeth Lev actually demonstrates how, at a crucial moment in the Church's history, artists used paintbrush and chisel to proclaim the gospel. This book will be extremely helpful for catechists, teachers, preachers, and, I daresay, for artists themselves."

—Bishop Robert Barron

"Elizabeth Lev's new book, beautifully produced by Sophia Press, is the first systematic effort in more than fifty years to organize the images and ideas of the Catholic Counter-Reformation and Baroque periods in narrative fashion. Legible and incisive, her text sheds light on the most influential development in Western sacred art after the Franciscan revolution of the late Middle Ages, helping modern readers reconnect with the dynamism of Catholic culture in the early modern era. Her volume is a must for teachers and students alike!"

—**Monsignor Timothy Verdon**
Director, Florence Cathedral Museum (Italy)

"This is a work not only about beauty but of beauty. It will captivate those who love art, love the Faith, love great writing, or love all three. Great art and artists gave a powerful response to the whitewashed iconoclasm of the Reformation, but for us to profit from their visual theology, we need someone to open our eyes to behold their works, and the Faith they depict, in all their splendor. Elizabeth Lev, one of the best and most passionate guides to Christian art, provides those glasses."

—**Father Roger J. Landry**
Author, National Chaplain, Catholic Voices USA

Elizabeth Lev is one of the foremost art historians and experts on the city of Rome. In *How Catholic Art Saved the Faith*, she skillfully shows how one of the most effective responses to the Protestant Reformation was not argument, but art. The splendid works of Catholic art are not just beautiful; they also evangelize and bring us closer to Jesus by revealing truth. In this insightful and compelling book, you will come away with an even greater appreciation for the way in which the art of the Catholic Reformation not only responded to a difficult challenge, but also deepened the faith of countless generations of Catholics, up until today.

—**Timothy Michael Cardinal Dolan**

HOW CATHOLIC ART
SAVED THE FAITH

ELIZABETH LEV

HOW
CATHOLIC ART
SAVED *the* FAITH

———————— ❖ ————————

*The Triumph of
Beauty and Truth in
Counter-Reformation Art*

SOPHIA INSTITUTE PRESS
MANCHESTER, NEW HAMPSHIRE

CONTENTS

Part III

COOPERATION

INTRODUCTION

Caravaggio may seem the most unlikely choice to spearhead a public-relations campaign for the Catholic Church. This aggressive, unconventional artist rarely followed rules—whether legal or artistic—and was more frequently under arrest than in Eucharistic adoration. Yet this brilliant painter joined several other "misfit" artists—hypochondriac Barocci, alcoholic Annibale Carracci, gritty Ribera, and scandal-ridden Artemisia Gentileschi—to become the visual-arts SWAT team of the Catholic Church in an age of crisis, the post-Reformation era.

A dark and divisive cloud swept through Europe in the wake of October 31, 1517, when Martin Luther's Ninety-Five Theses challenged almost every aspect of the Faith. Confusion reigned supreme regarding everything from the sacraments, which accompanied human beings from birth to death, to the saints, who set daily examples in the liturgical calendar. Was Jesus present in the Eucharist? Could the procession of historical Christian heroes in Heaven assist the living? Was Mary's role in the story of salvation solely that of the "God bearer," with no lasting influence over the Church?

As these questions of faith took a geopolitical turn toward issues of power, the debate grew increasingly ugly. Harsh language disseminated through the printing press was supplemented by vicious images, such as Lucas Cranach's *Passionary of Christ and The Antichrist* series from 1521, where thirteen woodcuts showing scenes from the life of Christ were contrasted with those of the Antichrist, represented as the Roman pontiff. Violence escalated, dialogue broke down, and brother turned against brother as the wars of religion began. What could calm these storm-tossed waters?

The arts.

Pope Emeritus Benedict XVI repeated both as cardinal and as Roman pontiff that "art and the saints are the greatest apologetic for our faith."[1] The Catholic Church of the Counter-Reformation relied on this premise as it unleashed a wave of glorious examples of holiness as well as beautiful sacred art in opposition to the ugliness, confusion, betrayal, and loss rampant in that era. Artists, despite their personal obstacles toward sanctification, were recruited to teach, delight, and inspire through their gifts, and complement the hallowed lives of Charles Borromeo, Ignatius of Loyola, Philip Neri, Thomas More, Teresa of Avila, and Jane Frances de Chantal, who shone as examples of spiritual beauty.

Initially perhaps, self-interest may have motivated artists. The menace of iconoclasm, a side effect of the Protestant Reformation, saw paintings, statues, and relics destroyed in several

---

[1] Benedict XVI, Address to Clergy of Bolzano-Bressanone, August 6, 2008, https://w2.vatican.va/content/benedict-xvi/en/speeches/2008/august/documents/hf_ben-xvi_spe_20080806_clero-bressanone.html.

pockets of Northern Europe, and was gaining ground in the south. Painters and sculptors were in part to blame for the hostility toward images. Enamored of their own prowess, some artists had lost sight of the holy stories in favor of provocation, often of a lascivious nature, or else a vain virtuosity, arraying a dizzying number of figures but masking the sacred message. This period, dubbed ineffectually by art historians as Mannerism, gave the world the notion of "art for art's sake" that would take on a life of its own in the eighteenth century. For the post-Reformation era, however, the watchword was something else entirely: "art for faith's sake."

It is not surprising that, faced with promiscuous or confusing images, some Catholic prelates questioned the wisdom of continued art patronage while the Church was preparing to reexamine her teachings in the Council of Trent. Music, literature, and the visual arts were under scrutiny as to whether the pleasure they provided was merely profane delight instead of a stimulus toward piety and eternal salvation.

There was much to discuss in the Council of Trent, from sacraments to saints and Magisterium to mission. The two decades of intermittent meetings from 1545 to 1563 spanned five popes, the birth of ten religious orders, more than one hundred officially recognized martyrs, and the repercussions of the astounding volte-face of King Henry VIII, who decreed himself the head of the English church in 1534.

The Tridentine fathers, truth be told, spent far less time discussing art than art historians would like, but their decrees, of the twenty-fifth and final session of December 4, 1563, reaffirmed the long-standing relationship between art and faith, essentially restating the points made at the Second Council of Nicaea in 787. The Tridentine decrees were deliberated along with the role of relics, a precursor to Benedict XVI's observations on the power of the saintly and artistic beauty.

> The bishops shall carefully teach this: that, by means of the histories of the mysteries of our Redemption, portrayed by paintings or other representations, the people is instructed, and confirmed in [the habit of] remembering, and continually meditating upon the articles of faith; as also that great profit is derived from all sacred images, not only because the people are thereby admonished of the benefits and gifts bestowed upon them by Christ, but also because the miracles which God has performed by means of the saints, and their salutary examples, are set before the eyes of the faithful; so that they may give God thanks for those things, may order their own lives and manners in imitation of the saints, and may be excited to adore and love God, and to cultivate piety.[2]

By 1564, art patronage was secured, but the instructions were vague. How were artists to comply with these lofty and somewhat ambiguous expectations? The solution came in the form of a remarkable and unprecedented collaboration, that of prelates and painters. In the search to tell old stories for a new world and emphasize ancient truths for a modern generation, the Church sought out all types of artists: the edgy Caravaggio, the graceful Guido Reni, the technically perfect Annibale Carracci, the colorful Barocci, the theatrical Bernini, and the passionate Artemisia Gentileschi. Every creative soul, despite its interior struggles, was

---

[2] Council of Trent (hereafter Trent), *Canons and Decrees of the Council of Trent* (Rockford, IL: TAN Books and Publishers, 1978), 270–271.

invited to be a part of this great project of affirming salvation in the Catholic Church through beauty.

While artists knew how to wield the brush and chisel, interpreting sacred stories for the faithful was the province of preachers. The Church, despite the setbacks of the Mannerist era, decided to encourage these individual artistic visions, shaping them through formation. Prelates published an unprecedented number of artistic treatises in this era. Written in Italian, they aimed to help artists satisfy the requirements of the new age, and, in the words of Gabriele Paleotti, archbishop of Bologna, transform painters into "tacit preachers" with the "office to delight, teach, and move."[3] Artists were offered the status they had craved from the time of Leonardo da Vinci, but with that power came great responsibility in the care of those souls entrusted to their talents.

Amid the brutal martyrdoms, doctrinal uncertainty, and vitriolic language that filled the pamphlets churned out by the printing press, art provided a way to draw people together instead of tearing them apart. This was an age of unprecedented art patronage from the top down, effectively a very expensive PR campaign meant to awaken the hearts and minds of the millions of pilgrims who were making their way to the Eternal City. This mission continued into the next century, reaching its zenith during the era now called the Baroque. It lasted until the mid-eighteenth century, but eventually dwindled during the Enlightenment, when people turned away from religious art to the crumbled vestiges of the pagan past in search of truth and beauty.

---

[3] Gabriele Paleotti, *Discourse on Sacred and Profane Images*, ed. Paolo Prodi, trans. William McCuaig (Los Angeles, CA: Getty Research Institute, 2012), 309.

Which brings us to now. Centuries have passed since Church patronage produced the likes of a Caravaggio or a Bernini, and very few people commission church décor in fresco or oil paint these days. Why, in this era, should we be interested in the drawings and disputes of a bygone age?

The reason is that the challenges and circumstances that the Church faced five hundred years ago bear a striking similarity to the ones the faithful face today, while the truths of the Church that artists so deftly displayed half a millennium ago have remained the same. Even today, art can assist the Church with several of her needs:

1. *Art is useful in evangelization*, the mission of the Church and her faithful to telling the great story of our salvation. Just as Jesus told stories, Christians recount their personal witness. Artists can make stories, old and new, come alive in paint, marble, or, in this age, film.

2. *Art can bring clarity*. In a world of ambiguity and confusion, art allows for the serene discussion of different interpretations of events but can also provide guidance—the tradition of belief and the tradition of beauty go hand in hand, ultimately meeting in transcendentals: truth, beauty, and goodness.

3. *Art is uplifting*. The language of art affirmed Church teaching but also delighted the faithful and enjoyed a universality, thanks to the attraction of the beautiful. Artists of the post-Reformation era were encouraged to represent the best of humanity even in its worst moments.

Certainly, the written word, the sacraments, and the power of preaching form the core of the Church's mission, but art plays a very important role with people, who tend to privilege the gift of sight. As in the post-Reformation era, people today are accustomed to understanding and believing through the gift of vision. So, in a world where people prefer seeing the movie to reading the book, an artistic movement begun almost five hundred years ago can still aid the Church in her mission today.

This book presents the major challenges the Church faced during the age of the Protestant Reformation that were effectively answered through art and architecture. While some works date from the first response to Luther in the 1520s and a few others from late 1600s, most of the art discussed is the product of the immediate generations following the Council of Trent, from 1570 to 1650. Three sections are devoted to considering the issues of sacraments, intercession, and the role of human cooperation in salvation, as explored in art. Each section, in turn, contains seven chapters that look at specific issues and situations, and then present works of art created to address those issues. The final chapter is dedicated to Michelangelo's *Last Judgment*, the ultimate Catholic response to the Protestant Reformation, summing up the most essential doctrines of salvation and projecting them toward a glorious destiny intended by God for every living soul.

The art of this tumultuous period represented a concerted effort to reinforce ancient teaching with new pictures, confronting modern crises with images of eternal truths. The innovations of this period in art were less a reaction to the prodding of the Protestant Reformation and more a dynamic renewal of an engagement with the arts that had been going on since the third century. For this reason, instead of using the term *Counter-Reformation*, suggesting that the period was merely a reaction to the tumult of Martin Luther, John Calvin, and companions, this book will employ the term *Catholic Restoration* to emphasize that, after the shock of the early events, the Church proactively represented her ancient teaching through the powerful language of art.

Fundamentally, the beauty in these pages is the fruit of conflict, where the natural collides with the supernatural, the universal call to sainthood encounters humanity's fallen nature, the personal relationship with God confronts the mission of the universal Church, and man's desire for stability is threatened by the modern options that ever-expanding knowledge brings. The Church proposed that the most fruitful place for this debate, which ignites creativity like flint and tinder, was on canvas, not in the streets.

The works discussed in this book were primarily selected from the Italian peninsula. Although Spain and some of the Netherlands also produced magnificent art to reinforce Catholic tenets — particularly Marian teaching and Eucharistic theology — the closest collaboration between artists and theologians took place in the city-states of Italy: Florence, Venice, Milan, Naples, and Rome. Here, the post-Reformation era created a "terroir" where particular nutrients — popular piety, artistic excellence, public processions — created a fertile soil where many "varietals" could flourish, producing many different yet excellent "vintages."

Many of these works have found their way to museums all over the world, but some remain above the altars and in the chapels for which they were commissioned, so the reader might view this book as an invitation to a pilgrimage to see these works with the same eyes as the faithful who walked from city to city on their way to Rome for the great Jubilee Years.

It is my sincere hope that in reading this book, you will revel in meeting new artists and seeing new works of art, enjoy learning more about the painters you already knew, and take pride in the unique and extraordinary contribution to culture that the Catholic Church gave to art. Art of the Catholic Restoration was intended to delight and to teach (*delectere et docere*). It is my greatest hope that you will find both knowledge and pleasure in these pages.

Part I

THE SACRAMENTS

❖

Battles over bread, wine, water, oil, and salt sound more proper to the kitchen than to the Church, but the most pressing issue in the wake of the Protestant Reformation was that of the sacraments. Sacraments had been part of the Church's life from her origins, yet Protestants, constantly chipping away at the role of the "intermediary"—the clergy—revealed the deep confusion that had infected the faithful regarding the sacraments, especially those of the Eucharist and Penance. While Baptism, Marriage, and Extreme Unction punctuated the cardinal points of most human lives, the Eucharist and Penance appeared more abstract in the minds of many of the faithful, having been eclipsed by the obfuscating clouds of Protestant rhetoric.

"Sacraments are necessary for man's salvation," argued St. Thomas Aquinas in the thirteenth century, reiterating the ancient writings of St. Augustine. Instituted by Christ, they are a "hidden sanctity,"[4] its humble outward form concealing the power within.

---

[4] Thomas Aquinas, *Summa Theologica* III, q. 60, art. 1, and q. 61, art. 1.

The Fourth Lateran Council had defined the dogma of transubstantiation back in 1215 and mandated that the faithful receive Holy Communion and go to Confession at least once a year. But three hundred years later, the faithful still reluctantly received both Confession and Communion, often looking instead to obtain indulgences through pilgrimages and pious activities for the remittance of sins.

Distance from the sacraments and the ignorance surrounding them made for fertile ground for Luther in 1517. The first two of his Ninety-Five theses attacked the sacrament of Reconciliation directly:

1. When our Lord and Master Jesus Christ said, "Repent" (Matt. 4:17), he willed the entire life of believers to be one of repentance.

2. This word cannot be understood as referring to the sacrament of penance, that is, confession and satisfaction, as administered by the clergy.[5]

Much of the ensuing confusion could be attributed to an erratically educated clergy, often unable to answer the increasingly pointed questions put to them by the faithful, now faced with belief "options." Another, more insidious problem, however, plagued the orthodoxy of the Church: clergy who were sympathetic to the Protestants. Martin Luther's support for married clergy quickly won over many Italian clerics, not least in the religious orders.

Therefore, Lutheranism owed its spread not only to the printing press but also to Catholic public preaching. One anonymous

---

[5] *Martin Luther's 95 Theses: With the Pertinent Documents from the History of the Reformation*, ed. Kurt Aland (Saint Louis, MO: Concordia Publishing House, 1967), 1.

commentator in the mid-sixteenth century claimed that several preachers from Catholic religious orders appeared to be the "authors of the present heresies."[6] Other orators used a subtler rhetoric, omitting the essential Church teachings on the questions of the sacraments and giving the illusion of compatibility between Protestant beliefs and Roman Catholic doctrine. Other Catholic intellectuals chose to straddle the fence: Erasmus of Rotterdam remained strikingly mealy-mouthed about Penance, leaving the question up to Scripture scholars.[7]

Explaining sacraments to the faithful grew even more difficult in the aftermath of the Reformation. While virtually no Christian doubted the divine institution and importance of Baptism, the other six sacraments were debated even among the different factions of the Protestants. Despite his rejection of Penance, Luther affirmed the Real Presence of Christ in the Eucharistic species, and King Henry VIII had personally penned the *Defense of the Seven Sacraments*. But by the mid-sixteenth century Henry had broken with Rome, and, despite his attempt to maintain the sacraments, in 1563 his successor, Queen Elizabeth I, ratified the Thirty-Nine Articles of Religion, which, while maintaining the importance of the Eucharist, declared: "Those five commonly called Sacraments, that is to say, Confirmation, Penance, Orders, Matrimony, and Extreme Unction, are not to be counted for Sacraments of the Gospel, being such

---

[6] Paolo Prodi, *Il Cardinale Gabriele Paleotti (1522–1597)*, 2 vols., Uomini e Dottrine (Roma: Edizioni di storia e letteratura, 1959), 173.

[7] Giorgio Caravale, *Preaching and Inquisition in Renaissance Italy: Words on Trial*, trans. Frank Gordon, Catholic Christendom, 1300–1700 (Leiden: Brill, 2016), 76.

as have grown partly of the corrupt following of the Apostles."[8] Meanwhile Ulrich Zwingli, parting ways with Martin Luther, argued that the Eucharist was merely a sign, claiming he had no use for any notion of a real and true body that does not exist physically, definitely, and distinctly in some place.

Faced with alternate doctrines and a clergy often unable or unwilling to clarify the situation to the baffled faithful, this increasingly empirical society, accustomed to understanding through sight and touch, grew skeptical toward the Real Presence of Christ in the Eucharist.

The Council of Trent tackled these issues head-on, reaffirming the ancient teaching based on Scripture and Tradition. The bulk of the sessions focused on the sacraments, particularly Penance and the Eucharist, asserting not only the Real Presence and sacramental Confession, but also expressing deep concern for the spiritual well-being of the faithful, contaminated as they were by incorrect teaching.

Session VII in 1547 under Pope Paul III acted "in order to destroy the errors and extirpate the heresies that in our stormy times are directed against the most holy sacraments, some of which are a revival of heresies long ago condemned by our Fathers, while others are of recent origin, all of which are exceedingly detrimental to the purity of the Catholic Church and the salvation of souls."[9]

Such decrees were clear and powerful and were even read aloud to the public in the large piazzas, but the question remained:

---

[8] William Baker, A Plain Exposition of the Thirty-Nine Articles of the Church of England (London: Francis and John Rivington, 1883), 145.

[9] Trent, Canons and Decrees, 82.

How to reawaken the faithful to the Eucharist? How to stimulate an increasingly literate population who had been inundated with theories, pamphlets, and information discrediting the Church to experience a relationship with Christ through the sacraments?

Enter the arts.

Art, meant to stimulate emotion through color, line, and space, spoke to the faithful on a deeper level than mere abstract argument. As reason alone revealed itself insufficient to grasp a mystery such as the Eucharist, the Church adopted beauty to open the minds and hearts of believers. It had worked in the past—one need only think of the Eucharistic hymns of St. Thomas Aquinas or the majestic cathedral of Orvieto, built to house the relics of Italy's most famous Eucharistic miracle—and it would become even more effective in this era.

Accustomed to seeing images in churches all their lives and exceptionally skilled at reading them, the believing public of the late sixteenth century may have found words confounding, but the comfort of the sacred space was filled with the faces of old, holy friends. The gentle, bearded Christ, the lovely veiled Virgin, the scarlet-swathed, golden-haired Mary Magdalene, and the wrinkled, wise St. Jerome reassured the faithful as a theological treatise could not.

These ancient role models were given new costumes and stage sets, with more dramatic parts to play. These great saints who had lived and died in the Faith or for the Faith made extraordinarily effective witnesses for truth. The debates of the present called upon these witnesses from the past, and artists were expected to close the gap of the centuries between those lives and the present age through the employment of their prowess.

Artists were not alone in this endeavor, however. "Art must be free" came much later, as a mantra of the Romantic era, bent on sweeping away the last vestiges of the faith-driven art of the preceding centuries. The artists of the Catholic Restoration still worked side by side with prelates and theologians, who could not only provide advice and inspiration in tackling the sacred stories but could also get the works placed in the most public places — the churches. The role of the artist grew along with his responsibility to the point where, in the words of Cardinal Gabriele Paleotti of Bologna, they were to be "mute theologians"[10] in preaching to the faithful, the highest status of intellectual life in the age.

The spiritual insight of Charles Borromeo, Robert Bellarmine, Federico Borromeo, St. Philip Neri, and Paleotti fused with the creative talents of Caravaggio, Barocci, the Carracci School, Lavinia Fontana, and Guido Reni, making for a heady cocktail designed to entice the faithful into experiencing mystery.

[10] Paleotti, *Discourse on Sacred and Profane Images*, 309.

Chapter 1

THE EUCHARIST AND THE SPACE OF MYSTERY

—————— ⁜ ——————

Churches have always been the privileged locus for experiencing and learning about the Faith. Starting with the first legally constructed cathedral, St. John Lateran, built in 324 after Emperor Constantine's Edict of Milan permitted Christians to practice their Faith openly, church design was carefully curated. Latin crosses or Greek crosses—each design both evangelized and evoked the mystery of the sacraments, while the décor served to enhance the fundamental lessons laid out by the structural plan.

Unfortunately, the medieval era, concerned with decorum, had created elaborate barriers known as rood screens—gated walls between the faithful and the sanctuary—which enhanced the mysterious nature of the Eucharist but also created a sense of detachment from the sacrament. Then, by the time the Renaissance era dawned, architects and patrons had grown so obsessed with classical designs that the centrally planned churches seemed to focus more on man than on God.

The post-Tridentine Church was concerned with establishing a more intimate relationship between the faithful and the sacraments, particularly the Eucharist. Infrequent Communion and garbled teaching had already distanced the faithful from the Body and Blood of Christ. Furthermore, the obstacle of the rood screens and the distractions of individual altars, placed not only in side chapels, but also cluttering the nave on pilasters and columns, undermined the sense of focus that the earliest churches had kept toward the main altar, where the drama of salvation was being sacramentally re-presented.

The urgent task of the post-Tridentine Church was to reignite love for the Eucharist: regular, even daily reception of Holy Communion was encouraged, provoking acrimonious debate. The Forty Hours devotion began around the same time as the Council of Trent and by the end of the council, thanks in no small part to Sts. Ignatius of Loyola, Philip Neri, and Charles Borromeo, the practice had spread such that, in 1592, Pope Clement VIII declared that the entire city of Rome should adopt the "Forty Hours, with an arrangement of churches and times such that, at every hour of the day and night, the whole year round, the incense of prayer shall ascend without intermission before the face of the Lord."[11]

This reinvigorated focus on the Eucharist swept through churches like a gust of fresh air. Screens were removed, private altars and devotional spaces were cleared away to help the faithful focus entirely on the high altar of the church. New churches were built, and, in the older churches, special chapels were constructed to house the Blessed Sacrament.

---

[11] John A. Hardon, *The History of Eucharistic Adoration: Development of Doctrine in the Catholic Church* (Oak Lawn, IL: CMJ Marian Publishers, 1991), 10.

The first great architectural impetus of the Catholic Restoration took place in Rome thanks to an energetic pope, an erudite cardinal, and an enterprising religious order.

Past Meets Present: The Gesù Church in Rome

The Gesù, the first new church to be constructed in Rome after the Reformation, was the artistic fruit of Pope Paul III's family wealth, St. Charles Borromeo's writings, and the eleven-year-old fledgling Society of Jesus, founded by St. Ignatius of Loyola.

Charles Borromeo, archbishop of Milan, was nephew to Pope Pius IV and had assiduously followed the final sessions of the council. Beyond his holy example and exceptional learning, Borromeo took an interest in ecclesiastical architecture. His treatise *Instructiones Fabricae et Supellectilis Ecclesiasticae* applied the decrees and concerns of the Council of Trent to the design and decoration of Catholic churches and was so successful that it was reprinted nineteen times, up to 1952. Although the treatise was intended for his own diocese, St. Charles's close association with the Jesuit Order ensured that the mother church of the Jesuits, the Gesù, begun in 1568, would become the atelier for his ideas.

Footing the bill for this new edifice was Borromeo's old adversary, Cardinal Alessandro Farnese, grandson of Pope Paul III and one of the richest in the college of cardinals. In a beautiful twist of providence, both Cardinal Farnese and Cardinal Borromeo commenced their ecclesiastical careers as wealthy, worldly men, but during the turbulent years after the Reformation, each experienced an intense personal conversion. Together, they would leave a beautiful, lasting, educational memorial to the centrality of the Eucharist in the glorious Roman Church of the Gesù.

Church of the Gesù, Rome, façade

The Gesù set out to focus the congregation on the sacrament of the Eucharist. The architectural challenge was so stimulating that even the aged Michelangelo had offered his assistance free of charge, but the task fell to Farnese's house architect: Giacomo Barozzi da Vignola.[12] The majestic travertine façade, with its powerful stability, borrowed from the example of ancient Roman structures, declared its purpose as the receptacle of the ineffable Lord. The disproportionately small doors—uneven in number,

---

[12] Giulio Carlo Argan and Bruno Contardi, *Michelangelo Architect* (London: Thames and Hudson, 1993), 341.

since Borromeo wished to create a focus on the center—made for an awe-inspiring first impression as one entered the soaring space crowned with the innovative high barrel vault.

The Gesù was the first church in Rome in over a millennium to be built without a rood screen. In response to their empirical age, Borromeo and the Tridentine fathers encouraged the faithful to gaze upon the Host and witness the Consecration. The entire design of the Gesù drew the eye uninterruptedly from door to altar, like the lens of the soon-to-be-invented telescope.

Where physical separation of the screens had grown into spiritual separation from the Eucharist, the new designs invited the faithful to Communion. A low rail replaced the screen, gathering the people around the Body of Christ, instead of leaving them outside. Reinforcing St. Ignatius's methods in the *Spiritual Exercises*, where the composition of place invited the senses to participate in prayer, the Gesù invited the laity to taste, touch, see, hear, and smell the presence of the Lord.

The apse containing the tabernacle sat in a direct sightline from the door. The goal of the arduous journey of life, represented since ancient times by the long nave leading to the sanctuary, beckoned from the entrance. Made of precious stone—a temple within the temple—the tabernacle was raised on steps, so that, just as Moses encountered the Lord on Sinai, and just as Jesus was transfigured at Tabor and redeemed mankind on Golgotha, so one had to climb to reach the Body of Christ.

The Gesù's crossing, the intersection of the transept and the nave, was surmounted by a dome, the first in Rome after that of St. Peter's (which at the time was still unfinished). Lifting their eyes after Communion toward the lofty cupola, which seemed to float above the large windows, the faithful caught a glimpse of the desired union of which the Tridentine fathers spoke: "After the

Church of the Gesù, Rome, main nave and altar

journeying of this miserable pilgrimage, [the faithful] will be able to arrive at their heavenly country, there to eat, without any veil, that same bread of angels which they now eat under the sacred veils."[13]

Giovanni Battista Gaulli, a protégé of the brilliant Gian Lorenzo Bernini, decorated the dome and vault of the Gesù, using art to pull back the veil of man's mortal vision to reveal the heavenly celebration that is the Mass.

SIDE CHAPELS: ARCHITECTURAL POLYPHONY

The side chapels, instrumental in proclaiming the efficacy of the Sacrifice of the Mass for the souls of the departed, as reaffirmed by Trent, received careful attention.[14] United by doorways, the chapels also served as side aisles, leaving the main path of the nave unimpeded. Uniform in size, the chapels eschewed the Renaissance penchant for allocating larger spaces according to status, as well as avoiding the temptation to self-glorification in personalized chapel dedications, by preselecting the dedications as part of a larger program.

The chapels in the Gesù emphasized the decorative and spiritual theme of the whole basilica, as the harmonies of Giovanni Pierluigi da Palestrina's sacred music enhanced his melodies, without ever obscuring the prayerful words of the Mass.

The Gesù plan was intended to guide the communicant from the church entrance to the altar and then back out into the world again. Paired left and right across the nave, the chapels closest to the main altar start with the intangible: the Trinity and the orders of angels, decorated by the giants of Catholic Restoration art Jacopo Bassano and Federico Zuccari.

---

[13] Trent, *Canons and Decrees*, 112–113.
[14] Ibid., 189.

The next chapel commemorates the historical reality of the Incarnation and is paired with the deeply moving Chapel of the Passion by Gaspare Celio. At the entrance, the prophets Isaiah and Zechariah entreat the viewer to "see thy teacher" and to "look on him whom they have thrust through."[15] Surrounding the altar are four images of Christ, exposed to public view during His Passion, when the crowd, blind to the presence of the Son of God, chose to beat, ridicule, and condemn Him to crucifixion. Seeing with the eyes matters, but more so does seeing with the soul.

The weight of witness marks the final chapels, originally dedicated to the apostles and to the martyrs. Placed by the exit doors, they summon those who have seen and experienced the truth of Christ, as do we when we participate in the sacrifice of the Mass, to "go therefore and make disciples of all nations" (Matt. 28:19).

BETWEEN HEAVEN AND EARTH: THE TABERNACLE

Hard on the heels of the Gesù came the first purpose-built Blessed Sacrament chapel in a papal basilica, St. Mary Major. Although Eucharistic adoration dated back to the early Church, some Reformers had criticized the practice as idolatry. On the contrary, the Tridentine fathers believed that the more time the faithful spent in the presence of the Lord, the better. Tradition has it that St. Francis of Assisi introduced the practice of adoration to Italy (certainly he lived in the same century as the establishment of the feast of Corpus Domini in 1264); thus, it seems appropriate

---

[15] Gauvin A. Bailey, *Between Renaissance and Baroque: Jesuit Art in Rome, 1565–1610* (Toronto: University of Toronto Press, 1999), 187–260.

that a Franciscan pope would build a glorious chapel expressly for that purpose.

Charles Borromeo had intended that new churches be focused on the Eucharist, but the requirements of *Caeremoniale Episcoporum* prohibited reservation of the Eucharist on the high altar of cathedrals and churches in which pontifical ceremonies were to be performed, so papal basilicas such as St. Mary Major needed a separate space for the exposed host.[16] Pope Sixtus V (reigned 1585–1590) responded by constructing his burial chapel around the tabernacle.

This Sistine Chapel, named for its founder, formed a beautiful enclosure intended to deepen the faithful's experience of Christ's Body and Blood. Shaped as a Greek cross, the chapel was surmounted by a large dome, reminiscent of that of St. Peter's by Michelangelo, which was being completed at the same time. Papal architect Domenico Fontana performed the remarkable feat of sinking an ancient shrine already in the church, containing a precious relic of Christ's crib, into the crypt of the chapel. In this same subterranean area, the pope placed the remains of St. Jerome, who had died in Bethlehem in the cave where Jesus was born. The pope completed the ornamentation of the chapel with one of the earliest nativity sets ever carved, made by Arnolfo di Cambio in 1291. In the dark little grotto, under the lofty, luminous dome, Pope Sixtus recreated the moment of the Incarnation, much as St. Francis had done 350 years earlier while preaching in Greccio.

---

[16] Steven F. Ostrow, *Art and Spirituality in Counter-Reformation Rome: The Sistine and Pauline Chapels in S. Maria Maggiore*, Monuments of Papal Rome (Cambridge: Cambridge University Press, 1996), 17.

This tie between the Incarnation and the Eucharist had been especially reinforced at Trent, where the fathers decreed: "We believe that same God to be present therein, of whom the eternal Father, when introducing Him into the world, says: And let all the angels of God adore him whom the Magi falling down, adored; who, in fine, as the Scripture testifies, was adored by the apostles in Galilee."[17]

Above the crypt, sculptors Bastiano Torrigiano and Ludovico del Duca cast the six-and-a-half-foot-tall tabernacle in bronze, perching the massive temple-shaped monument on the shoulders of angels (also over six feet). The daring design conveyed an impression of weightlessness with the Sacred Host floating above the grotto below, seemingly suspended under the dome. In the cupola, frescoes of the celestial hierarchy drew the eye up to the image of God the Father at its apex. Sixtus's design was intended to illustrate the doctrine of transubstantiation, so hotly debated, by evoking Christ's physical participation with the world yet suffused with His divinity, through the bronze tabernacle, which appeared to hover between the cavern below and the heavens above.

The finest witness being example, Pope Sixtus chose to have his funerary statue, sculpted by Giovanni Antonio Paracca, not seated in authority or lying in state, but, in an innovative twist, on his knees, adoring the Body of Christ. In this way, Sixtus evoked not only the line attributed to St. Francis, "Preach always, when necessary use words," but also the first rule of the Franciscan Order: "Friars should receive the Body and Blood of our Lord with great humility and reverence."[18]

---

[17] Trent, *Canons and Decrees*, 110.
[18] Ostrow, *Art and Spirituality*, 18.

The impact of these pioneering structures on art would be powerful, inspiring beautiful new altarpieces to emphasize the importance of the Eucharist. Soon painters would take up the challenge and dedicate their creative talents to illustrating this sacramental mystery in fresco and oil.

Chapter 2

PAINTERS AND THE EUCHARIST

———————— ❖ ————————

Post-Tridentine Italy redesigned churches to lead the faithful
to the Eucharist, but that was only half the battle; one might
lead the sinner to the bread of life, but how to convince him
to believe in it? Yes, now they could see the Consecration; yes,
now they consumed the Host more regularly; but how to open
the eyes of the heart to the mystery of Christ's Real Presence?

Enter the painters.

Brandishing brushes, girded with personal faith, and flanked
by theologians, artists labored to ignite the imagination and
deepen devotion to the Eucharist in their increasingly empirical age.

Painters, grown expert at rendering the natural world during
the Renaissance, were now required to illustrate mystery. They
rose to the daunting challenge, at first proposing studied works
for sophisticated audiences before developing an ease with the
subject that drew even the uncultured viewer toward the Real
Presence. From Florentine Andrea del Sarto to Federico Fiori of
Urbino to Milanese Caravaggio to the Bolognese Domenichino,

painters would blaze a Eucharistic trail through the Italian peninsula, keeping pace with the new practice of adoration.

The Altar and the Body of Christ

Michelangelo had already set the stage with his Roman *Pietà*, commissioned in 1500 for St. Peter's Basilica. Mary grasps Jesus under the arm through what can be interpreted as a humeral veil, but her other hand releases the body, allowing it to slide toward the altar below, as if presenting the body of her Son to the sacrifice.[19] This composition paved the way for dozens of later images during the Catholic Restoration to underscore the Real Presence in the Eucharist.

A quarter century later, Andrea del Sarto, fleeing the plague, went to stay in a monastery nestled in the Tuscan countryside. There, in 1523, he painted a panel for the Church of St. Peter in Luco. As the epidemic attacked bodies and heresies poisoned souls, Andrea, in the quiet oasis of Luco, did his part to provide a spiritual antidote. His fellow Florentine, Pope Clement VII, elected that same year, had declared a month after his election that the heresies of Martin Luther were "the most serious issue of the day."[20] Andrea del Sarto became one of the first painters off the mark to provide artistic clarity to Catholic teaching on the Eucharist.

---

[19] Elizabeth Lev, "A Marian Interpretation of Michelangelo's Roman *Pietà*," in *Revisioning: Critical Methods of Seeing Christianity in the History of Art*, ed. James Romaine and Linda Stratford (Eugene, OR: Cascade Books, 2013), 214.

[20] Antonio Natali, "Andrea Del Sarto, a Model of Thought and Language," in *The Cinquecento in Florence: "Modern Manner" and Counter-Reformation*, ed. Carlo Falciani and Antonio Natali (Firenze: Mandragora, 2017), 92.

His *Lamentation over the Dead Christ*, commissioned by the powerful abbess Caterina di Tedaldo della Casa, is a powerful, packed, X-shaped composition that draws the eye inexorably to the body of the lifeless Christ. Giorgio Vasari, a contemporary, noted that Jesus "seems to be truly a real corpse."[21] The figures around Him are arrayed in lively colors, catching the eye, like the lilt of music, but their gestures always lead back to the grayish body in the center. St. Peter stands in front of rocks, alluding to the Magisterium, while St. Paul, Apostle to the Gentiles, has a cityscape behind him. The image, however, does not focus on them nor on the lovely Magdalene and Catherine of Alexandria (the namesake of the patroness).[22] Jesus is placed on a slab of stone, an obvious allusion to the altar, propped up on a white sheet. At the exact point where the chalice would be lifted before this altarpiece, Andrea del Sarto painted a golden paten, with a Host resting on its edge. The extraordinary capabilities of the painter allowed him to render the Host almost translucent, seemingly weightless with a faint cross inscribed on the side, even as Jesus' body appears to bear down on it. This beautiful rendition of transubstantiation was well suited to the visually sophisticated faithful of the Medici court.

The "Recipe" for the Eucharist

Andrea del Sarto's shimmering color served as inspiration for young Federico Fiori, also known as Barocci. This painter, who hailed from Urbino, the hometown of Raphael, developed the technique of "changing colors," which propelled him to stardom

---

[21] Giorgio Vasari, *The Lives of the Artists* (London: Penguin Books, 1965), 152.

[22] Natali, "Andrea Del Sarto," 92.

Lamentation over the Dead Christ, by Andrea del Sarto

during the Catholic Restoration. He delighted viewers with his variegated hues, all the while conveying his message with powerful drawing. Barocci was personally summoned in 1603 by Pope Clement VIII to decorate his parents' burial chapel in the church of Santa Maria sopra Minerva in Rome with the altarpiece of the *Institution of the Eucharist*. Pope Clement was so committed to the Eucharist that he often wept at the Consecration, carried the monstrance barefoot during the Corpus Domini processions, and established the continuous Forty Hours adoration in Rome in 1592.[23] He took a hands-on approach with the artist, in a working partnership aimed at rekindling in the faithful true devotion to the Blessed Sacrament.

The new post-Reformation iconography shifted attention away from the moment of Judas's betrayal—so frequently depicted in the *Last Suppers* of the Renaissance—and instead centered on the *Institution of the Eucharist*, when Jesus uttered the words of consecration for the first time. The great draftsman Barocci's drawings stimulated the mind, but his mastery of color employed surprising mix of hues to create what he described as "tuning his music."[24]

The composition is formed out of three triangles, the apex of each at the head of Christ. The first extends down to the lower corners of the canvas, where two young men are reaching toward the altar, as if to pick up the gifts presented there. The second triangle encompasses the kneeling Sts. Peter and John, to evoke the reverent prayers of consecration, now visible to the public after the removal of the rood screens. Jesus' arms form the final triangle, holding the Host above the red part of His robe, a symbol of His humanity. Pope Clement repeatedly weighed in on the painter's sketches, insisting that he make the Eucharist

---

[23] Torgil Magnuson, *Rome in the Age of Bernini*, 2 vols., Kungl Vitterhets, Historie Och Antikvitets Akademiens Handlingar Antikvariska Serien (Stockholm, Sweden: Almqvist and Wiksell International, 1986), 40.

[24] Giovanni Pietro Bellori et al., *The Lives of the Modern Painters, Sculptors and Architects* (New York: Cambridge University Press, 2005), 172.

The Institution of the Eucharist by Federico Barocci

more evident.[25] Barocci depicted a simple yet compelling "recipe" for the Eucharist—matter plus prayers becomes the Body and Blood of Christ.

THE INCUMBENT NECESSITY OF THE SACRAMENT

Michelangelo Merisi da Caravaggio was also catapulted to fame thanks to his Eucharistic imagery. Spotted by the newly formed congregation of the Oratorians, the troubled yet brilliant painter from Milan was commissioned in 1603 by Pietro Vittrice to paint an altarpiece in the recently renovated Roman church of Santa Maria in Vallicella. Though clearly influenced by Michelangelo's *Pietà*, Caravaggio's *Entombment* proposed the Real Presence in a strikingly updated way. Caravaggio's version arranged six figures in a triangular mound against a dark background. The accusations by his peers of "excessive naturalism" appear justified, looking at the aged Mary, Mother of God, the stocky Nicodemus, and the dirty feet of Christ. Those, however, are the only naturalistic elements in the work: the figures are piled up without plausible spatial depth and the light has no natural source.

Against this darkness, supernatural light draws immediate attention to the gesticulating female figure at the summit of the composition. Whereas compositions usually lift the gaze upward, the extended hand of Caravaggio's female figure draws the focus toward the base of the canvas, where lies the altar. Following the arrangement of the figures, the viewer is almost compelled to bow physically before the Host.

The tumble of figures culminates in Christ, suspended above a stone slab, which, in turn, mirrors the altar below. His ungainly, lifeless body hangs heavily in midair, over a shadowy open space.

---

[25] Magnuson, *Age of Bernini*, 98.

The Entombment of Christ by Caravaggio

Caravaggio's peers considered it essential for artists to complete a composition, therefore leaving a gaping abyss in the painting would have immediately surprised contemporary viewers. But Caravaggio left this apparent lacuna to be filled by the priest celebrating Mass at the altar; when the celebrant recited the Eucharistic prayer, he would complete the picture. Building on Michelangelo's *Pietà*, in which the body of Jesus seems about to fall from Mary's lap to the altar, Caravaggio added a greater urgency to participate in the sacrament, as if the entire group in the painting were waiting for the faithful to step up and accept the offering made for mankind.

FOOD FOR THE JOURNEY

Rome owed the practice of the Forty Hours devotion to St. Philip Neri, who lived with the Confraternity of St. Jerome of Charity for thirty-three years before moving to Santa Maria in Vallicella. This confraternity devoted itself to burying the dead, ministering to prisoners, and celebrating eight Masses a day. In 1612, Cardinal Pietro Aldobrandini, nephew to the Eucharist-loving Clement VIII, commissioned the Bolognese painter Domenico Zampieri to paint the *Last Communion of St. Jerome* for the high altar of the confraternity's church.

St. Jerome, near death, is accompanied by an eclectic band comprising (among others) a woman, a turbaned man, and a figure recalling a Roman aristocrat. A youth with the long hair distinctive of the confraternity members lifts the dying saint toward the Host, as his grayed, crumpled limbs can no longer support him.

Rising above this turbulent sea of humanity stands the priest, holding the Host moments after the Consecration. The deep bows of the priest, the deacon, and the subdeacon, evoke the

The Last Communion of St. Jerome by Domenichino

solemn dignity of the Lord's presence amid the chaotic suffering of life. Jerome's eyes awaken as he gazes upon the Host, the shining passage to eternity, represented by the floating angels coming to claim his soul.

A jealous rival accused Domenichino of plagiarism, and the resulting scandal has obscured the unique quality of this piece — the emphasis and focus on the Eucharist, awakening the inner life of the spirit even as the physical life fades away.

The paintings by Domenichino, Caravaggio, and Andrea del Sarto were deemed artistic masterpieces by Napoleon's commission of the arts, so in 1797, when the Corsican general conquered Italy, he looted these works (among many others) and had them brought to Paris. There, these altarpieces became war booty effectively stripped of their religious meaning, a glorious backdrop for the triumphal parade before Napoleon's coronation.

Returned in 1815, they are well preserved but still displayed away from their original altars, their message muted by clinical assessments of style and form. Only Barocci's canvas remains in its original setting, able to enhance the infrequent liturgies before it by illuminating mystery.

Chapter 3

PRELATES, PENANCE, AND PAINTERS

The logical consequence of more frequent Communion was increased confessions. The emphasis on a more regular participation in the Eucharist carried with it a responsibility to be prepared to receive the Lord. St. Charles Borromeo reasoned that "those who receive communion more often confess more often" and as a result "have fewer and smaller sins."[26] The emphasis on these two sacraments in the post-Reformation era would intensify the personal relationship between the faithful and God.

Not without a battle, however, Martin Luther inflamed hearts and minds with his energetic attacks on the sacrament of Penance. Laying the blame on priests whose "perilous and perverse doctrine" had divided "penitence into three parts, contrition, confession, and satisfaction," Luther claimed that they had "taken

---

[26] *Charles Borromeo: Selected Orations, Homilies and Writings*, ed. John R. Cihak, trans. Ansgar Santogrossi (London: Bloomsbury, 2017), 71.

away all that was good in each of these and have set up in each their own tyranny and caprice."[27]

The sacrament of Penance was so crucial to the Church that it rallied twice to the defense of Confession during the Council of Trent. First, it denounced the Reformers' Doctrine of Justification in 1547 and in the fourteenth session, in 1551, the Council Fathers meticulously explained the divine origin of Penance, its necessity, and its fruits. The necessity of a priest to administer the sacrament was also underscored in canon VI of the same session.

> If any one denies either that sacramental confession was instituted or is necessary to salvation, of divine right; or says, that the manner of confessing secretly to a priest alone, which the Church has ever observed from the beginning, and does observe, is alien from the institution and command of Christ, and is a human invention; let him be anathema.[28]

The fifteen decrees rejected Protestant heresies and clearly established Catholic teaching, but the difficulty came in translating the dogmatic statements into the daily life of the faithful. Again, the Catholic Church looked to art not only to teach but also to invite people to partake of this sacrament.

This presented a new challenge to art. The confessional was feared for harsh penances or as a "slaughter-house of conscience,"[29] and art was asked to emphasize the essential role of the clergy in

---

[27] Martin Luther, "On the Babylonish Captivity of the Church," Christian Classics Ethereal Library, https://www.ccel.org/ccel/luther/first_prin.v.iii.html, 185.
[28] Trent, *Canons and Decrees*, 139–140.
[29] Ibid., 131.

the auricular sacrament of penance, as opposed to the Protestant view of confession as silent prayer, discussion with a trusted friend, or admitting guilt to one who has been wronged.

Ecclesiastical patrons, directly affected by these decrees, initiated a dynamic exchange with artists, resulting in poignant works destined mostly for intimate settings. The earliest paintings were intended to excite penitential devotion first and foremost among the clergy, who were supposed to lead by example.

St. Robert Bellarmine, Jesuit priest, theologian, and, perhaps most famously, antagonist of Galileo Galilei, spent much of his life refuting the Protestant heresies in his massive literary project *Disputationes de Controversiis Christianae Fidei*. The book, known in English as *The Controversies*, systematically argues everything from indulgences to angels to the alleged Pope Joan. It was intended to assist the educated clergy to refute heretical teachings as well as urban legends. St. Robert Bellarmine dedicated a significant section to the three pillars of the sacrament of Penance, which were particularly denigrated by the Protestants: contrition, confession, and satisfaction. Painters, therefore, had three choices for exploring the sacrament in art.

St. Peter, Model of Contrition

Who better to lead the iconographic charge to contrition than penitent St. Peter? He had denied Christ three times, and yet it was to this apostle that the keys to bind and loose souls were entrusted. Peter became the model of the contrite heart in scores of portraits painted by artists such as El Greco, Ribera, Van Dyck, and Guercino. Bolognese painter Guido Reni (1575–1642) became a specialist in depicting the Prince of the Apostles, producing more than a dozen portraits of him. Never destined to hang in a church, they graced the private setting of a prelate's home. They aimed at inciting emulation of the leader of the apostolic band not only as visible head of the Church, but especially in his humble acknowledgment of his sins before the Lord.

Reni's most famous penitent Peter now hangs in a museum but was intended for private meditation. Produced around 1600, when the Jubilee Year preached conversion throughout Europe, this early work by Reni featured looser, more visible brushstrokes to capture the immediacy of the apostle's call to contrition. Peter is depicted as the same size as the viewer, with no background or distraction to alleviate the sorrowful scene. The work is like a mirror, inviting the prelate to imitate the example set by the first pope.

Reni brightly illuminated Peter's bared chest, directing the eye to linger on the exposed flesh, as Peter opens his heart. His hand, splayed across his skin, evokes the dramatic gestures favored in this period, but also recalls the physical rebuke during the Confiteor of "*Mea culpa, mea culpa, mea maxima culpa.*"

The wiry strands of his beard and the chiaroscuro crevasses of his wrinkles add a kinetic force to Peter's contrition, and even as he submits himself humbly to divine justice, his recognition of sin is active. His face turns upward toward the source of light, hopeful in forgiveness, as tears well up in his eyes and fall down his cheek. This intimate portrait of repentance puts forward a model of contrition that could speak persuasively to the proud world of Roman clerics.

ART IN THE SERVICE OF CONFESSION

Another giant of clerical reform was St. Charles Borromeo, archbishop of Milan. He encouraged each of the priests of his diocese, especially those with the mandate to preach, to "first

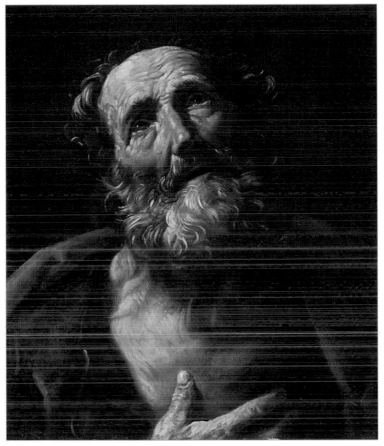

St. Peter Penitent by Guido Reni

purge his conscience of all impurity of sin by the Sacrament of Penance."[30] To that end, in 1564 he designed a space within the church intended for the hearing of confessions, today known as confessionals.

[30] *Charles Borromeo: Selected Orations*, 87.

The very definition of sin grew blurred in the Reformation as John Calvin denied a difference between mortal and venial sin.[31] Listing sins, classifying sins, seemed to the Reformers a pernicious activity despite its biblical foundations in the First Letter of St. John. After all, offending the all-pure God was an infinite offense whether in the form of adultery or an uncharitable word. To counter the Reformers' tracts, the figure of the priest sought to guide the soul in understanding the gravity of one's sins, in a special space reserved for that form of discernment.

The beautiful confessional by Giovanni Taurini in the Jesuit church of San Fedele in Milan is a particularly exquisite execution of Borromeo's plan. Carved from walnut wood, the box featured open sides for penitents and a center section for the confessor. Little grills separating the priest from the penitents answered the need for both privacy and propriety.

The style was so successful that Pope Paul V adopted the form in his Roman Ritual, so one can still find these confessionals everywhere in Rome, from the gigantic St. Peter's to the tiny San Carlino alle Quattro Fontane on the Quirinal Hill.

Together with the altar, the tabernacle, and the baptismal font, the sacrament of Penance was given its own special architectural space within the church, underscoring its importance as a sacrament.

DEMANDING SATISFACTION

The final element of Reconciliation was that of satisfaction, or the penances undertaken by those whose sins were forgiven. The Protestants held this practice in particular contempt, so

---

[31] John Calvin and Henry Beveridge, *Institutes of the Christian Religion* (Grand Rapids, MI: Wm. B. Eerdmans, 1989), 520.

Confessional in San Fedele, Milan, carved by Giovanni Taurini

the Church not only recruited artists to illustrate the ancient tradition of penitential activity but also adopted St. Jerome as the penitent par excellence.[32]

Luther had denied St. Jerome's claim that penance was a "plank for those who have had the misfortune to be shipwrecked," losing baptismal innocence.[33] But this Church Father who inflicted hard penances and lived for years in the worldly courts of Rome before taking up the penitential life in the desert and translating Scripture into Latin was not so easily silenced. St. Jerome had translated Scripture more than a millennium before Luther, and his example of humble service repudiated Protestant pride. During the magnificent era of the Renaissance, Jerome had been depicted as an elegant figure in an ornate study, but the Catholic Restoration transformed him into a penitential hero to be immortalized by Caravaggio, the Carracci, and Veronese, among many others.

Of the numerous versions to choose from, Barocci's *St. Jerome* in the Galleria Borghese bears closer investigation. Out in a wilderness, the saint kneels in his cave. The sun is setting in the distance, but Jerome has his lantern to continue his work into the night. The ground is hard, the wicker basket scratchy, and the sparse vegetation offers little sign of life.

Jerome holds a crucifix before his eyes as he grasps a stone, preparing to inflict blows on his body in mortification. It is doubtful that the medieval beholder found these images of self-inflicted punishments any more attractive than the modern viewer.[34] They

---

[32] Marcia B. Hall, *After Raphael: Painting in Central Italy in the Sixteenth Century* (Cambridge: Cambridge University Press, 1999), 272.

[33] Jerome, Epistle 130: To Demetrias.

[34] *Charles Borromeo: Selected Orations*, 8.

St. Jerome by Federico Barocci

served a valuable purpose, however: "These penitential practices, which seem rather severe today, can also be interpreted as a positive response to the dissolute times."[35] Symbols of the passage of time, from the hourglass to the skull, remind the viewer that all are ultimately called to give an accounting of themselves.

It is Barocci's brushwork that renders the image so captivating. The rose-colored mantle billows and falls, catching the light. Like the body about to bruise and bleed, the cloth evokes energy. The swells of cloth are rendered in broad, quick strokes, while Jerome's face seems to be the result of high-definition photography. The tiny bristles crisply delineate the aged features of the saint — fine wrinkles, swollen eyelids, parted lips — yet the hoary visage of the elderly man is belied by his fervent expression as he gazes upon the crucifix, his burden lightened by his fiery love of Christ.

The array of examples of clerical penitence paved the way for new commissions directed at the faithful to draw them more closely to the sacrament of Penance. Soon, models of Peter and Jerome gave way to new figures to incite the faithful to contrition, confession, and satisfaction.

[35] Ibid.

Chapter 4

CONFESSION AND THE LAITY

———————— ❖ ————————

"Sin and sin boldly," Martin Luther exhorted Philip Melanchthon in 1521, when his collaborator wavered over the Reformation's rejection of penances, and he reminded him to "let your trust in Christ be stronger."[36] In his enthusiasm, Luther promised that justification was so great that "no sin can separate us from Him, even if we were to kill or commit adultery thousands of times each day."[37]

These words resounded powerfully through a world where the proud achievers of the Renaissance grew tired of the humiliating, messy, and often downright ugly practice of confronting one's sins in the confessional. The Catholic Restoration urgently needed to reawaken the desire for Penance and penitential practices among the faithful, but it needed to do so by lifting up rather than beating down. In this case, as with the Eucharist before,

---

[36] Martin Luther, "Let Your Sins Be Strong: A Letter from Luther to Melanchthon, Letter No. 99," in *The Wartburg (Segment) from Dr. Martin Luthers Saemmtliche Schriften* (St. Louis: Concordia Publishing House, 1521), cols. 2585–2590.

[37] Ibid.

art came to the rescue by proposing models of confession and contrition that would stimulate the faithful to emulate them.

PAINTING THE FIRST CONFESSION

Titian produced one of the very first such models in 1566, just three years after the close of the Council of Trent. A Venetian, Titian had come to Rome to work for Pope Paul III in 1546, the year after the opening of the council, and he attended one of the sessions on the topic of Penance.[38] As a young man, he had earned wealth and fame by delighting Europe with his sensual mythologies and haughty portraits. But the mature Titian had also suffered great losses, including the successive deaths of his wife, daughter, and grandchild. He produced fewer erotic scenes and began to focus on images of Christ and His Crucifixion.

Titian painted *Christ and the Good Thief* as part of a sixteen-foot-high painting of the Crucifixion, but this startling composition made the object of his focus the very image of the sacrament of Confession.

The composition excludes the bad thief, who has chosen to reject and mock Christ. Instead, Jesus and the good thief are raised high above the spears of the Roman soldiers, even as the darkness of death encroaches.

The good thief, impelled by a sudden hope, finds the strength to speak and to raise his hand in supplication. Confessing his guilt — "we are receiving the due reward of our deeds; but this man has done nothing wrong" — he finds mercy, as Christ, almost dead Himself, promises, "Today you will be with me in Paradise"

---

[38] A painting, attributed to Titian, of one of the council meetings hangs in the Louvre museum.

Christ and the Good Thief by Titian

(Luke 23:40–43). His penance paid on the cross, the thief is able to die in peace.

Titian captures the intimacy of this moment as if in a confessional. The thief is turned toward the Lord, the light that awakens him, while Christ is turned sideways as in the sacrament, without shaming the penitent. The daring perspective not only isolates the two figures in the powerful moment of redemption, but Jesus' outflung arm invites us, too, to share our sins with Him, to shoulder our penance and bask in the warmth of His mercy. Titian's sensuality, so often employed to portray mythological bedchambers, creates a compelling atmosphere for this monumental example of Confession.

TRANSFORMING THE SENSUAL INTO THE SPIRITUAL

The conversion from sensual to spiritual was a favorite theme of the imagery of penance. A life of self-indulgence acknowledged, repented, and atoned for, garnered particularly high regard in these years. St. Margaret of Cortona played a key role in inviting the faithful to penance, especially since the sacrament had played such a dramatic role in her own life. Born in 1247, the beautiful, willful Tuscan native enjoyed using her beguiling charm to win attention. At seventeen, she chose to run off with a nobleman, who kept her as his mistress without marrying her. She bore him a child out of wedlock, only to discover his murdered body a short time afterward.

The shock of seeing the body awoke her soul to the horror of death in mortal sin. Her contrition was immediate, and she was so convinced that she must make a full confession of her sins that upon her return home, where her father hoped the incident could just be forgotten, Margaret publicly admitted her guilt and was thrown out of her family's house, with all the resulting shame.

She was taken in by the Franciscans, and after three years of fasting and other penances, she eventually joined their third order. Far from being hidden away, as her father had hoped, Margaret lived in the public eye, founding a hospital and inspiring others, and on one occasion she even dared to rebuke a bishop for his worldly ways. Dante Alighieri, then a young poet celebrated for his romantic verses who was soon to turn to writing the epic *Divine Comedy*, is believed to have visited the holy woman.

"I have put you as a burning light to enlighten those who sit in the darkness," Jesus said to her during one of her ecstasies, "so that they might see, through your example, how my mercy awaits

St. Margaret of Cortona by Guercino

the sinner who is willing to repent."[39] The devotion to Margaret of Cortona began upon her death in 1297 and flourished in the seventeenth century, though she wasn't canonized until 1728.

Painted for the Capuchins of Cesena, a town in the Papal States, Guercino's 1648 St. Margaret of Cortona compellingly illustrates the positive effects of penance. Guercino depicts very little in the way of setting: a simple room with a stone floor, a wooden dais, and an altar barely visible on the right. In the little sliver of lapis blue, one can make out a church in the distance: it is the church of St. Basil, where the body of the saint had become an object of devotion and pilgrimage. The curving line of the penitential rope she wears knotted around her waist leads the eye to her clasped hands and to her upturned face, bathed in the glow of the heavens. We cannot see Christ, with whom she converses, but she can. The sacraments—Confession and Communion—are what turned her life from sin and intensified her relationship with God.

INTIMACY THROUGH CONFESSION

Intimate. Personal. Transformative. The power of penitence was lost on the Reformers, especially as they grew prouder and increasingly involved with worldly affairs. The Church, however, wanted to encourage Confession as a means to accompany souls, like a coach training an athlete.

St. Philip Neri, one of the most beloved figures of the Catholic Restoration, converted the hearts of the vain noblemen of Rome and then strengthened them through Confession. Wealthy, pampered, proud youths flocked to him, and he used humor and

---

[39] Alban Goodier, Saints for Sinners (New York: Image Books, 1959), 21.

truth to win them over. Each of his legendary penances — such as ordering a self-absorbed aristocrat to walk through the city carrying an ugly dog or telling someone to gather the scattered feathers from a ripped pillow to illustrate the dangers of gossip — was attuned to instruct the penitent and help him grow stronger in faith.

The intensely personal nature of Confession was beautifully depicted by Annibale Carracci in his *Christ Crowned with Thorns*. Painted for Cardinal Odoardo Farnese in 1598, the image offered a moving testimony to the effects of sin, confession, and mercy. It was so successful that dozens of copies were made of the work, some by famous artists.

Christ, crowned with thorns, is shown as if through a window, where the figures are the size of the viewer. The painting stands out for the inescapable intimacy of the scene — only three faces are represented, instead of the usual throngs that encircle Christ. They fill the space, making it impossible for the viewer to escape first-person involvement in this moment. Christ's tormentors are concealed by shadows as one affixes the crown of thorns on Christ's head. Another dimly lit man stands behind Christ, his helmet glinting in the darkness as he summons the other soldiers to join the taunting.

Jesus, exhausted from the flagellation, is subjected to renewed torment. The Roman soldiers, their cruelty still not spent, drape the Lord in a purple robe and crown Him "King of the Jews." Mocking his victim, the soldier in the foreground aggressively thrusts his finger in Jesus' face while gingerly placing the sharp ring of thorns on His head.

Christ's head is at the heart of the canvas, not tall and majestic, but bent low toward the soldier. Jesus responds to the wagging finger by lifting His bound hands toward the man in a gesture of

Christ Crowned with Thorns by Annibale Carracci

friendship and brotherhood. Christ's face, blood-spattered and showing exhaustion, nonetheless glows with a warm radiance. He responds to the taunts with a gentle expression; no anger or menace here. The viewer is taken aback at this astonishing example of charity.

The open space in the foreground of the composition makes us uncomfortably present, a reminder that those thorns that bite into His flesh are the sins of mankind. His slender fingers seem to hover toward the beholder, aware of the viewer even while absorbed by His tormentor.

One might imagine that the soldier leaning toward Christ would be spitting and laughing as he hailed the "King of the Jews," while Jesus, gently clasping his persecutor's shoulder, would whisper, "I am doing this for you because I love you."

In viewing this work, one can almost hear, smell, and sense every detail of the moment. But Annibale's version of the mocking of Christ is more than just a realistic narrative; it is a call to greatness of spirit. The viewer must ask himself, "Is He reaching for the jailer or for me?" Either way, the message is clear: no one is beyond repentance and no one is beyond redemption.

Chapter 5

MARY MAGDALENE: MAKING
PENANCE LOOK GOOD

The Reformers stigmatized confession with words like "impious," "Tyranny," "pestilence," "perversion," "monstrosity," and "butchery." With such brutal epithets, how could the Church convince the faithful of the inherent beauty of coming clean with the Lord and being renewed by His forgiveness?

Artists had always loved to produce depictions of Mary Magdalene. Not only was this woman the "Apostle to the Apostles," but she was also, thanks to a homily by Pope Gregory the Great, the ultimate model of repentance. In his Homily 33 on the Gospels, Pope Gregory conflated Mary Magdalene with several nameless women of the New Testament, including the prostitute who washed Christ's feet with her tears. This theological giant declared, "Whenever I ponder the penitential spirit of Mary Magdalene, I feel more like weeping than like speaking."[40] Realizing that her example would pave the way for others, he wrote, "The tears of

---

[40] Gregory the Great, *Forty Gospel Homilies*, trans. David Hurst, Cistercian Studies Series (Kalamazoo, MI: Cistercian Publications, 1990), 268–279.

this sinful woman will soften even a heart of stone toward the idea of doing penance. Having reflected on what she had done, she did not wish to set bounds to what she should do."[41] Far from shaming this great saint, as modern interpreters claim, he held Mary Magdalene up to be a beacon of penance for men and women alike.

Much like St. Jerome for prelates, Mary Magdalene never went out of style; she just changed costumes to suit the evangelical needs of the Church. A richly robed noblewoman in the Middle Ages, she became the passionate mourner under the Cross in the Renaissance and then returned in the Catholic Restoration as the glamorous model for penitence.

In this era, Mary Magdalene attracted many famous followers, including the noblewoman-turned-saint Maria Maddalena de' Pazzi and the extraordinary poetess Vittoria Colonna, so admired by Michelangelo. Colonna not only wrote a series of sonnets to the saint, but she also acquired Titian's startlingly lovely *Penitent Magdalene*.

Mary Magdalene reigned supreme in post-Reformation iconography, painted by Carracci, Caravaggio, and most every other major artist. No longer portrayed as an elegant aristocrat or an emaciated zealot, she became a sensuous figure, whose evident beauty and attraction were no longer directed toward the things of this world but were employed to inspire the faithful to the wonders of Heaven. Nor was she a dumpy creature, swathed in concealing robes with no attractions to conceal—the Magdalene was beautiful, but had dedicated her beauty to the service of God.

MODEL OF SELF-DENIAL

Of the many Mary Magdalenes Guido Reni painted, the version for Roman cardinal Antonio Santacroce was the most successful.

---

[41] Ibid.

St. Mary Magdalene by Guido Reni

The saint, wrapped in heavy draperies, reflects a sensuous warmth in her soft limbs, but instead of leading the viewer to impure thoughts, she redirects his gaze to heaven. The lower half of her body is enclosed by the gray stone of her cave, like a self-designated tomb. Her robe, instead of the usual fiery red, has been dulled with a cool blue to mauve, symbolizing through color the tempering of human passions. Roots lie by her side, indicative of her penitential fasts, while the cross and skull allude to her self-mortification, following the example of Christ. The upper part of her body appears warmer as her golden tresses part to reveal her luminous chest; Mary bares her heart to the Lord and, in doing so, becomes a beautiful depiction of the sacrament of Confession. Angels welcome and comfort her, opening the path to Heaven for this saint who makes penitence chic. Much as movie stars and models become advertisements for products of superficial beauty, Mary Magdalene became a poster child for an interior cosmetology.

MODEL OF REDISCOVERED CHASTITY

Mary Magdalene addressed the very human desire for worldly pleasures: sex, wealth, and the power that physical attraction wields. She became a key figure in the conversion of prostitutes. Particularly in sixteenth-century Rome, prostitution was an enormous problem. Convents for "converted women" — in particular, the convent of Mary Magdalene of the Converted, founded in 1520 near Piazza di Spagna in Rome — offered these women an opportunity to change their lives and save their souls. In 1622, Guercino was commissioned to paint *The Penitent Magdalene with Two Angels* for the high altar of the church.

Guercino did a great many paintings of penitents, from Margaret of Cortona to St. Peter to Mary Magdalene, but this version was special. The saint is portrayed kneeling before Christ's

The Penitent Magdalene with Two Angels by Guercino

tomb, which bears a resemblance to the stone slab of an altar. Her shoulder is bare and her hair is loose, but no highlights shimmer to attract the eye, and her skin lacks the pinkish tinge that suggests voluptuousness. Indeed, the illumination of her neck and arm are to focus the eye on her hands, clasped in prayer.

She contemplates the holy nail and the crown of thorns, symbols of human sinfulness redeemed by Christ. The nervous movement of light and shade over her drapery, the angel's robes and the shroud, and the mesmerizing lapis blue, a signature color of the artist, highlight the intensity of her internal conversion, despite the stillness of her contemplative prayer. The world, its pleasures, and its possibilities are forgotten as the saint allows herself to be absorbed by the love of Christ.

The convent of the Convertite required that postulants be youthful and attractive, women who had chosen to leave their lives of sin, not those forced out because of lack of customers.[42] The penance and the conversion of these women was active and constant, the temptation to return to the old ways always present. Mary Magdalene illustrated to these women the attractiveness of conversion, allowing them to see themselves not as alluring to men, but beautiful before God. The angel looking out at the viewer leads the eye from the saint up to the heavenly cherubs, who indicate the presence of the Lord, extending the invitation to conversion into real time.

MODEL OF CONVERSION

The Catholic Restoration made Mary Magdalene a subject not only of art but of literature as well. Poet Marco Rosiglia recounted her conversion story in 1611, culminating in Jesus' passionate plea for her salvation. He pleads with her, "To give you a healthy, glorious life, I want to be flagellated and killed, so that you won't want to offend me anymore.... I want you for a sister ... and I am your Creator and your God."[43] Mary's response is to go home, strip off her gown and jewels, and repent, "so humble and lowly that she did not dare raise her eyes to heaven."[44]

[42] Pamela M. Jones, *Altarpieces and Their Viewers in the Churches of Rome from Caravaggio to Guido Reni*, Visual Culture in Early Modernity (Aldershot, England: Ashgate, 2008), 214.

[43] Ibid., 226.

[44] Ibid.

This powerful instant of conversion was captured by Caravaggio, the painter who would become famous for freezing the most dramatic moments in his art. His *Penitent Magdalene* was probably commissioned in 1595 by Pietro Vittrice, who would also commission *The Entombment* for the Chiesa Nuova a few years later. Closely connected with the Oratorians, Vittrice shared their focus on humility and contrition, so it is not surprising that Caravaggio was inspired to produce such a daring work.

Mary Magdalene is pictured seated, wearing a damask silk dress, an expensive and flashy outfit. Swathed around her is a yellow cloak, the article of clothing required by law to identify prostitutes. Caravaggio often used prostitutes as models, and the woman believed to have sat for this work, Anna Bianchini, was one of them, adding an unexpected touch of realism to the story.[45]

Mary's head is bowed, the milky-white skin of her neck exposed, revealing the vulnerability of this very intimate moment. The red sash around her waist suggests a woman bound by passions, but her arms cradle nothing but emptiness. Scattered on the floor are pearls, jewels, and a golden chain. The string of the pearls is broken, as she has just ripped them from her neck, casting away her worldly trappings. The first crystalline tear of repentance falls down her cheek, painted more delicately than the precious gems below. The jar of oil in the foreground evokes the "liter of costly perfumed oil made from genuine aromatic nard" with which she will anoint the feet of Jesus, drying them with her hair (John 12:3). This painting is often downplayed in Caravaggio's work because of the strange foreshortening, but one art historian has suggested that Caravaggio probably painted

<hr />

[45] Helen Langdon, *Caravaggio: A Life* (London: Pimlico, 1999), 149.

Penitent Magdalene by Caravaggio

the image while standing on a high ladder looking down at the model.[46] This God's-eye view of conversion, with the warm light bathing the weeping figure, suggests the Lord's delight in a soul that returns to Him.

[46] John L. Varriano, *Caravaggio: The Art of Realism* (University Park, PA: Pennsylvania State University Press, 2006), 9.

MODEL OF MORTIFICATION

For some artists, Mary Magdalene was more than a stock-in-trade character; she was also a real-life role model. Painter Agostino Carracci, whose early art was marked by secular, sensual, and often lascivious works, spent the last period of his short life in the convent of the Capuchins in Parma, where he painted a *Penitent St. Peter* and "devoted himself to the contemplation of God and heavenly things."[47] His oil-on-copper *Mary Magdalene* features golden hair and soft skin, but she sits with a rotted skull on her lap, its ghoulish grimace almost mocking her loveliness. She holds a discipline, showing the viewer that her flesh is bared to receive the harsh penance. The putto above holds a palm branch, usually the symbol of the martyr, indicating that this is how the worldly can cross the finish line of heaven without being slain for Christ. For Agostino, a fun-loving young artist who had to face death at age forty-two, this image was more than an academic subject; it was a personal model.

MODEL OF RENEWAL

One of the Catholic Restoration's most influential female painters also took an interest in Mary Magdalene. Artemisia Gentileschi experienced the pain of public transgression after she was raped at seventeen by her father's colleague and then allowed the relationship to continue, hoping he might marry her and repair her reputation. Her father's discovery of the situation and the subsequent rape trial humiliated and exposed the young girl to more gossip than the most scandalous of modern celebrities. Picking up the shreds of her life and packing up her prodigious

---

[47] Bellori et al., *Lives of the Modern Painters*, 121.

The Penitent Magdalene by Agostino Carracci

The Penitent Mary Magdalene by Artemisia Gentileschi

artistic talent, she moved to Florence to start again. She was propelled to fame thanks to the many beheading images she executed of biblical heroines, interpreted by modern feminists as her hatred of the man who ruined her and the patriarchal society that exiled her. These commentators, however, neglect to mention that Artemisia's second-most-popular subject was the penitent Mary Magdalene, perhaps addressing her unruly and occasionally scandalous personal life.

Artemisia, who broke new ground as the first female artist to join the Florentine art academy, painted a particularly moving Magdalene in 1617 for the Medici family. Like Caravaggio's Magdalene, she wears the yellow robe of a courtesan and sits amid luxurious silk and velvets. But she turns away from the gilded cage of delights, and her nude shoulders seem to emerge from the opulent trappings like a newborn reaching toward the light above. One hand is on her heart, which has been opened, the other reaches toward the mirror, revealing herself before God. Her eyes, now fully open, yearn for freedom, for Christ, for light. Her bare foot prepares for her first humble step toward a life of penitence. Mary Magdalene doesn't stop being beautiful or compelling when she turns to Christ, but that beauty is no longer meant to enrich herself but to glorify the Lord, who loves her more than anyone ever had. The Catholic Restoration propelled Mary Magdalene to iconic status, inviting everyone to throw off the heavy cloak of sin and bask in the light of redemption.

Chapter 6

BAPTISMAL BATTLES

————————— ❖ —————————

Baptism, the sacrament par excellence since the earliest days of Christianity, never came under the same virulent attacks during the Reformation as did the Eucharist and Penance. Confusion still reigned, however, when it came to the question of the effects of Baptism. Some Reformers held that the cleansing of sin in Baptism was enough to remit all sins committed from that moment onward.

One result of this dissension was the debate over the correct age for Baptism. Ulrich Zwingli, who would go on to found the Anabaptists, rejected infant Baptism, while more extreme denominations insisted that one be baptized at the same age as Christ when He died, thirty-three years. Infant Baptism remained the norm, however, among Catholics and most Protestants, but the Roman Church laid a different emphasis on the importance of that gift. The Catholic Church denied that Baptism would shield the faithful from punishment for all future sins, requiring Catholics to work constantly at maintaining the purity of the baptismal state through prayer, penance, and indulgences. Session 7 of the Council of Trent reiterated that after Baptism the faithful were nonetheless obliged to observe "all the precepts, whether written or transmitted, of holy Church."[48]

Rome, as the privileged destination for pilgrims in search of plenary indulgences that provided the opportunity to return to the debtless state of Baptism, sought to underscore the gift that is Baptism and the importance of maintaining that gift as pure and pristine as possible.

FROM THE BAPTISMAL FONT TO THE FOUNTAINS OF ROME

Pope Sixtus V came up with a delightful solution to entice the faithful to keep the law of Christ and follow the path that Baptism laid out for them: water fountains. The popes, as rulers of Rome, were responsible for the urban planning of the city. As thousands of visitors and pilgrims wandered through the streets, the papacy sought to help them navigate the dense streets to find their destinations. Attentive to the physical health of the flock as well as its spiritual salvation, Pope Sixtus V implemented in the Eternal City the first straight road system, punctuated by fountains.

Not only did Pope Sixtus build the Blessed Sacrament Chapel in the basilica of St. Mary Major, but he also completed St. Peter's Basilica (to Michelangelo's plan), moved the obelisk to where it stands today in St. Peter's Square, and redesigned the urban layout of Rome (all in a five-year pontificate!). He also paid special attention to the entry gates of the city, concerned about the first impression the Eternal City would make on pilgrims and visitors. Most travelers came from the north, so Sixtus singled out two principal entry points for renovation: Piazza del Popolo, where 80 percent of visitors arrived, and the Porta Pia,

[48] Trent, *Canons and Decrees*, 86.

close to St. Mary Major. The Porta Pia, designed by Michelangelo and sponsored by St. Pius V, was a gateway in the ancient Aurelian Walls, built to ease access into the city. The unsuspecting pilgrim, however, traversed the high gate only to find an uninhabited area of fields and thickets. Thanks to Sixtus, as of 1587 the disoriented traveler would see a straight road that led toward a large piazza. There, he would find the ancient church of Santa Susanna (rebuilt during Sixtus's pontificate) and the colossal remains of the Baths of Diocletian (Christian persecutor extraordinaire), which had been converted twenty years earlier into the Church of St. Mary of the Martyrs.

The weary, thirsty pilgrim would also be astounded to see a large travertine fountain, pouring cool, refreshing water to slake his thirst and bathe his dusty hands and feet. This gift of pure water greeted the pilgrim upon entering Rome, not unlike the gift of Baptism, given after a child entered the world. Sixtus's fountain made the comparison more explicit, however, by featuring Moses striking water from a rock.

This image had been associated with Baptism from the time of the early Church Fathers. Paleo-Christian art, which was being rediscovered in the catacombs during this time, abounded with images of Moses striking the rock. St. John Chrysostom, one of the early Fathers to link Moses and Baptism, also noted: "The sins committed after baptism require much energy so that they may again be cancelled. Since there is no second baptism, there is need of our tears, repentance, confession, almsgiving, prayer, and every other kind of reverence."[49] Sixtus's fountains

---

[49] St. John Chrysostom, *Baptismal Instructions*, trans. Paul W. Harkins, Ancient Christian Writers (Westminster, MD: Newman Press, 1963), 240.

restored physical energy, so the faithful could set about their spiritual duties.

Domenico Fontana, Sixtus's favorite architect, engineered the twenty-two-mile aqueduct to source the water. Named the Acqua Felice for the pope's given name, it was the second to be rebuilt in the city after the fall of the empire. The aptly named Fontana (the name means "fountain") chose white travertine for the project, a majestic stone associated with the architecture of old, particularly the triumphal arches of Roman military victories. Fontana designed the fountain with the same triple arcade motif, appropriating the pagan language of triumph to laud the victory over sin and death in Baptism.

The two reliefs on the left and right, sculpted by G. B. della Porta and Flaminio Vacca, illustrate scenes of Aaron, brother of Moses, leading his people to water and Gideons selecting his soldiers by their manner of drinking, but the gigantic statue of Moses dominates the whole. The sculptor, Prospero da Brescia, was brutally mocked for the disproportionate size and the anachronism of Moses holding the tablets of the law, which were given to him many years after the act of bringing forth water, but, in fact, this was not an oversight on the part of the artist or the Scripture-scholar pope. Mighty Moses, while symbolizing the act of Baptism, carries the law that must be followed, as emphasized in the canons of Trent. Breaking that law brings with it the need for repentance through its many forms, including pilgrimage.

Sixtus's fountain may have been denigrated for its ungainliness, but his work spawned many more. From the later copy on the Janiculum to the Trevi Fountain, the city flowed with water, subtly, or in the case of Sixtus's Moses, overtly, reminding people of their baptismal vows.

Renewing Baptismal Vows and Views

Even timeworn subjects were renewed during the era following the Reformation. Certainly, there was no lack of images of Jesus' Baptism in art. From mosaics crowning the baptisteries in Ravenna, to the cycles of the life of Christ executed everywhere from the Scrovegni Chapel to the Sistine Chapel, not to mention the towering statue groups, such as the one produced by Andrea Sansovino in 1505 for the baptistery of Florence, it is safe to say that every denizen of the Italian peninsula was familiar with the iconography of the Lord's Baptism. Everyone could recognize the regal Jesus, standing erect and visibly strong, clearly the leader and master of the scene. John, by contrast, was mostly portrayed as the emaciated zealot, next to Jesus' more muscular form.

Hubris led many of the Protestant Reformers astray, a pride that was contrasted by the humility of many great saints, from Charles Borromeo to Philip Neri. These men held up the example of Christ, who divested Himself of heavenly glory and came in the humble guise of man to redeem. This humility, a fundamental element in recognizing oneself as a follower of Christ, became an iconographic fixture in images of Jesus' Baptism.

Annibale Carracci's *Baptism of Christ* was painted in 1584 for the church of Sts. Gregory and Siro in Bologna. In this altarpiece, Annibale portrayed the body of Christ bending forward toward the altar as His gaze falls on the cross held by John the Baptist in front of Him. This Baptism is the first public step of His mission that will lead Him to Calvary. Jesus' hands are crossed over His chest, as seen in the images of Mary at the Annunciation, when she offers herself as the servant of the Lord (see Luke 1:38). The obedience demonstrated by Christ becomes the new center of focus in versions of the scene produced during the Catholic Restoration. In the background, parents bring their naked newborn to the river, underscoring the Catholic practice of infant Baptism, while on the left, two young men compete for our attention. One is dressed in the pure white robe of the neophyte, symbolic of baptismal purity; the second, kneeling in the foreground, looks intently out at the viewer while pointing toward Christ.

One particularly interesting tidbit tucked into Annibale's work is the strange hairstyle of John the Baptist. The dramatically receding hairline on either side of his brow reflects a bright light. This little detail unites John to Moses, "the skin of [whose]

The Baptism of Christ by Annibale Carracci

face shone" from having been in the presence of the Lord (Exod. 34:29).

Baptism Goes Global

The Catholic Restoration saint most associated with Baptism is Francis Xavier. One of St. Ignatius's first companions, this charming Spanish student responded to a call within his Jesuit vocation to evangelize in the East. His journeys would take him tens of thousands of miles, and he is believed to have baptized more than one hundred thousand people. The relic of the arm that blessed so many souls eventually made its way to Rome and is now housed in the Church of the Gesù. Slowly, as the century progressed, the number of images of St. Francis Xavier in the act of baptizing began to rival those of John. These works captured the spirit of the age: the call to conversion and the dazzling possibilities of evangelizing an ever-expanding world.

Luca Giordano, the prolific Neapolitan painter who applied the artistic concepts of the Catholic Restoration to kingdoms that were lagging, produced a dazzling altarpiece in 1680 for the Gesù Church in Naples. *St. Francis Xavier Baptizing Proselytes* contains a mad jumble of people, sweeping the viewer up in a variety of colors and costumes. The image alludes to the account of St. Francis Xavier's conversion of Queen Neachile of India, who had initially been an implacable enemy to Christianity. In Giordano's work she is the luminous figure kneeling before the saint with her hands clasped in prayer as the water spills over them. Neachile, in turn, converted the other members of her family, depicted as turbaned figures, to the Christian God. From this coterie at the apex of the composition, the gift of Baptism flows to every person in the painting, regardless of skin color or age, as seen in the child offered by the mother below. A fellow Jesuit kneels in prayer on

St. Francis Xavier Baptizing Proselytes by Luca Giordano

the lower right, weapons of war and trappings of power discarded at his knees. As once Ignatius converted from being a soldier, so his followers go out into the world effecting conversions and sealing them with the sacrament of Baptism.

Chapter 7

HOLY ORDERS AND
RELIGIOUS CONSECRATION

———————— ❖ ————————

St. Peter, the prince of the apostles and the first pope, proclaimed, "Like living stones be yourselves built into a spiritual house, to be a holy priesthood, to offer spiritual sacrifices acceptable to God through Jesus Christ" (1 Pet. 2:5). Why then, the Reformers asked, had the Roman Church constructed a clerical hierarchy? If St. Paul, Apostle to the Gentiles, had written that Jesus, having sacrificed His body for our sins, by one offering "has perfected for all time those who are sanctified" (Heb. 10:14), what need was there for the tangle of abbots, prelates, bishops, and pastors littering the path of the faithful toward the Lord?

Indeed, many priests, "the tin gods and buffoons of this world," as derided by Luther, who, for his part, had thrown off his religious habit of an Augustinian friar, had been part of what made the terrain fertile for the Protestant Reformers.[50] Too many of the faithful had encountered worldly priests, collecting wealth

---

[50] *Luther's Works on CD-ROM*, vol. 36, *Word and Sacrament*, ed. Abdel Ross Wentz, 2nd ed. (Philadelphia: Fortress Press, 2001), "The Misuse of the Mass 1521," 140.

or pleasures. Sexual incontinence was rampant among Renaissance clergy, and their ignorance of Church teaching and history had shaken the trust that the faithful had placed in the clerical caste for centuries.

While the extensive clerical reforms decreed by the Council of Trent provided the most important solutions to these problems, art, too, played a key role in restoring respect for the image of the servants of God. Gifted artists lent their talents to depict the most extraordinary saints and to remind the faithful of the beautiful witness of holy priests and devout religious.

THE APOSTLE OF POLAND

The first saint to be canonized under the newly formed Congregation for Canonization of Saints, created after the Council of Trent, was Hyacinth of Poland, O.P. Born in 1185 to a noble family, Hyacinth received the greatest privileges in life: wealth, status, and an excellent education. Upon meeting St. Dominic, however, he chose to leave his comforts behind and enter the new mendicant order. For thirty-five years, Hyacinth put his great education and his enthusiastic faith to work, establishing many Dominican convents throughout Eastern Europe. Pope Clement VIII canonized this "Apostle of Poland," as Hyacinth was called in 1594, and the Dominican Order dedicated a chapel to him in its ancient church of Santa Sabina in Rome. To celebrate the Jubilee Year of 1600, they hired the celebrated painter Federico Zuccari to fresco the side walls of the chapel.

Zuccari painted two scenes from Hyacinth's life: his receiving his Dominican habit and his canonization. Arranged so as to face each other across the chapel, the stories represented the cardinal points of the saint's mission. The *Clothing of St. Hyacinth* is a meticulously structured scene, with the saint at the center

The Clothing of St. Hyacinth by Taddeo Zuccari

turned away from the viewer while he accepts the habit from St. Dominic. The viewer stands behind the new religious, as one would during the liturgy. Dominican priests line the wall, looking on with approval at the young man about to join their ranks.

Zuccari employs dramatic foreshortening, a favored device of gifted draftsmen, to stretch another postulant, lying facedown, toward the viewer. It is so carefully rendered that the soles of his feet are visible. He is closest to the entry point of the chapel, an open invitation to any others who might be discerning a vocation. On the left, a bishop embodies the hierarchy of the Church, watching over the investiture. Depicted in sharp profile, the prelate is there to represent ecclesiastical authority.

Lay people occupy the foreground and provide an illuminating contrast among themselves. Near the bishop, members of Hyacinth's family kneel calmly before the scene, accepting the decision of the young aristocrat. On the opposite side, several young men seem agitated; one even looks back with a question-ing expression. Through these brightly colored, eye-catching figures, Zuccari does more than exalt Holy Orders; he also en-courages laypeople to encourage and not hinder vocations.

FROM THE BATTLEFIELD TO THE BENEDICTINES

Twenty years later, Guercino revisited the topic of receiving Holy Orders on a monumental scale with his altarpiece of *St. William of Gellone*, painted for the Church of Sts. Gregory and Siro in Bologna (the same church where Annibale Carracci's *Baptism* was placed).

St. William takes the priesthood further back in time, to the age of Charlemagne. The Duke of Aquitaine, William repelled the Saracen advance in southern France, protecting Christen-dom from the Islamic invasion that had already claimed Spain. As soon as his heroic duties were done, he gave up the sword and dedicated his life to the Faith, joining the Benedictine Order.

St. William's return to fame was due, in part, to the rise of the Jesuit Order. Like William, St. Ignatius had been a heroic soldier and had also been called to the service of God. The rigorous military training they underwent resurfaced as the two saints took on more stringent ascetic practices. The discipline necessary to train the mind and subdue the body resembled that of the professional soldier. St. Ignatius's new order drew young men who would be willing to give up glamour and glory and "acting without motives of power or gain ... help others by their sound doctrine and good example."[51]

---

[51] St. Ignatius, of Loyola, *Personal Writings: Reminiscences, Spiritual Diary, Select Letters Including the Text of the Spiritual Exercises*,

In 1600, Caravaggio had introduced the use of chiaroscuro, the play of light and shadow, to heighten the drama of his scenes, and twenty-nine-year-old Guercino used this technique to brilliant effect in this mighty altarpiece of St. *William Receiving the Habit.* St. William towers above the viewer, despite being lower than the other figures in the scene. All lines lead to the dashing young man, clean-shaven and clad in glinting armor as he kneels before the bishop, relinquishing his sword moments before the folds of his habit falls over his body, erasing the military man of action and replacing him with the obedient man of God. A soldier and a monk converse easily on the right, regarding the similarities of the obedience, discipline, and rigor that mark their professions. The faces of two young acolytes peek out between the bishop and the saint. One gazes in admiration at the noble hero, while the other directs his eyes to the heavens, where the Christ, the Blessed Virgin, and two saints rejoice in the renewal of the priesthood. The example set by William will bear fruit in the hearts of these youths.

THE PRIEST AMONG THE PEOPLE

The importance of priestly ministry was also advertised in art of the Catholic Restoration. About the time Guercino was producing the painting of St. William, Carlo Saraceni was painting *St. Charles Borromeo Blessing a Leper* for the Servite Church in nearby Cesena. Saraceni, a Venetian, came to Rome during the exciting pre-Jubilee era in 1598 and, like Guercino, fell under the spell of Caravaggio's chiaroscuro technique. The beam of light illuminating the central figures reveals this old

---

ed. and trans. Philip Endean and Joseph A. Munitiz (London: Penguin Books, 1996), 236.

St. William of Aquitaine Receiving the Cowl by Guercino

enchantment, but over the years, Saraceni was influenced by a new type of imagery derived from Dutch realism, marked by meticulous detail. Saraceni anticipated the art of photography by two centuries, capturing surfaces, faces, and materials with exceptional precision.

The subject of Sarceni's painting is St. Charles Borromeo, the saint so committed to priestly reform that he was nearly assassinated by his own rebellious Milanese clergy for enforcing the requirements of obedience, poverty, and chastity. Sareceni depicts him visiting the plague victims in his city, the ultimate commitment of a shepherd staying with his flock. The saint, his features faithfully rendered, enters the dark chamber of a moribund young man, bringing with him the light of the Viaticum. The boy turns on the bed, his body covered in a russet blanket,

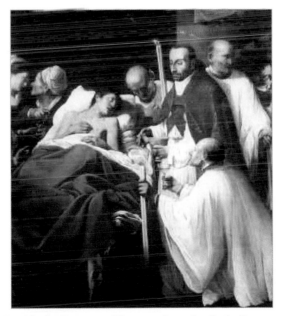

St. Charles Borromeo Blessing a Leper by Carlo Saraceni

vibrant in contrast with his skin, whose color drains away like the life from his limbs. His face however, resting against the bright white sheet, looks at the figure of the priest, risking his life to bring him the Lord one last time. St. Charles's mantle shines blood red, representing his active willingness to face anything from plague to assassination to fulfill his priestly service. Amazed family members marvel at the bravery of this intrepid band of clerics, while another group in the upper right waits for their visit and the consolation of the sacraments.

Saraceni and his patrons the Servites had perhaps the most successful depiction to remind the faithful of the importance of Holy Orders. The heroic journey of St. Charles Borromeo to the dying struck a chord deep in the collective memory. While many people were willing to debate the necessity of priests for Communion and Confession, in the frightening and lonely final journey of death most people looked for a priest.

Part II

INTERCESSION

❋

The Protestant Reformers disrupted ancient relationships between the natural and supernatural and the living and the dead when they attacked the veneration of saints. Although neither Luther nor Zwingli would deny the heroic witness of the apostles or that of the many holy men and women through the ages, they did cast doubt on the role the saints played in Heaven. That martyrs, confessors, teachers, and apostles were still active in Heaven, not only as role models for the living but also as intercessors in the faithful's path to holiness, was seen at best as a fairy tale and, in more extreme cases, as idolatry, where "dead saints were worshipped exactly in the manner in which of old the Israelites worshipped Baalim."[52]

The Protestants were conflicted about why saints could not intercede. Luther spoke of "soul sleep," in which "after death the soul goes to its bedchamber and to its peace, and while it is sleeping it does not realize its sleep, and God preserves indeed

[52] John Calvin, "Letter to Charles V on the Necessity of Reforming the Church" (1543), Protestant Heritage Press, http://www.swrb.com/newslett/actualNLs/NRC_ch02.htm.

the awakening soul."[53] Thus, if the soul of the saint is sleeping, how and why should it be troubled with cares of this world? Several Reformers chose to interpret the word "worship" regarding the saints and the Blessed Virgin as "adoration" rather than as "veneration," suggesting that Catholics were the same as the idolaters of old, and no different from the pagan Romans, Greeks, and other Gentiles. An even more insidious critique pointed out that most saints came from the ranks of the clergy, so devotion to the saints resembled a Hollywood awards ceremony, where people within the business glorified themselves by praising others in the same business.

These objections to the intercession of saints ripped a jagged fissure through Christendom. Protestant leaders and adherents, divorced from Catholic tradition, were not unanimous about intercessors. Luther continued to invoke the intercession of Mary in his early years, noting that "the veneration of Mary is inscribed in the very depths of the human heart."[54] The famous painter Albrecht Dürer, while sympathetic to the Protestant cause and friendly with the major figures of the Reformation, took comfort at the death of his mother in that she had "died in Christ with all the sacraments, absolved of punishment and guilt by papal authority," having received a plenary indulgence.[55] The rejec-

[53] Martin Luther, "Auslegung Des Ersten Buches Mose," in *Dr. Martin Luthers Sämtliche Schriften*, ed. Johann Georg Walch (St. Louis: Concordia, 1880–1910), vol. 1, cols. 1759, 1760.

[54] Martin Luther, "Sermon, September 8, 1522," in William Cole, "Was Luther a Devotee of Mary?" *Marian Studies* 21 (1970).

[55] David Price, *Albrecht Dürer's Renaissance: Humanism, Reformation, and the Art of Faith*, Studies in Medieval and Early Modern Civilization (Ann Arbor: University of Michigan Press, 2003), 22.

tion of the Roman Canon, the Eucharistic prayer used from the earliest age of the Church to invoke the saints at the altar during the re-presentation of Christ's sacrifice, made for a celebration of the Mass without guests.

The altarpieces that had represented the communion of saints present with Christ at the altar, figures with their familiar attributes who had become friends, confidants, and role models of the faithful, were suppressed. Relics, the physical reminders of the holy men and women who had struggled with sin, disabilities, setbacks, and doubt and had nonetheless lived glorious lives, were destroyed. Like removing athletic trophies from a sports club or the employee-of-the-month sign from the workplace, the myriad forms of extolling holy excellence were hidden from the faithful. Individualism became isolation, and the community of saints in Heaven and saints in waiting on earth was in danger of being permanently separated.

Interestingly, the Council of Trent addressed questions of intercession and veneration of saints in the same session as it did art and relics. Session 25, on December 4, 1564, the final meeting of the council fathers, decreed "that it is good and useful suppliantly to invoke them [the saints], and to have recourse to their prayers, aid, and help for obtaining benefits from God, through His Son, Jesus Christ our Lord, who is alone our Redeemer and Savior."[56] A few lines later, the council fathers went on to affirm the importance of the relics of these holy persons and the images that call to mind not only their great acts, but also their presence before God to intercede for the living.

As the lives of saints had made visible, albeit imperfectly, the kingdom of Heaven on earth, so art, within its own limitations,

[56] Trent, *Canons and Decrees*, 270.

could offer a glimpse of mystery, of history, and of the divine. Artists vied to excel at the task of renovating hagiographic iconography, the art of portraying the saints. From the static, old-fashioned "sacred conversations" of the Renaissance, featuring several saints gathered around the Madonna and Child, models of holiness became active in their invocations: kneeling, reaching, levitating, seeing both into this world and beyond it into the next. Artists, already challenged by an empirical society accustomed to seeing and touching and learning from the senses, used their creative vision to help the viewer see more than what nature allowed them to observe in the temporal world. Art invited the beholder to glimpse the supernatural. Guardian angels, ecstatic saints, souls in Purgatory, the onslaught of demons and all the forces of evil countered by the power of heavenly intercessors, awakened the faithful to the limitations of the earthly senses to perceive the invisible reality all around them.

Thanks to the newly mastered medium of oil paint, artists could replicate nature with almost photographic precision, but in the midst of their realistic details, they inserted supernatural events. Light and dark were employed to reveal what is of this world and what is of the next. The artist's toolbox was plumbed and often enlarged to find new ways of using perspective, foreshortening, brushstroke, and light to enhance the relationship between the faithful and the saints.

Mary occupied a special place in these battles. The Blessed Mother had entered the lives of the faithful as confidante, mother, sister, and generous advocate. *Madonnelle* — popular Marian icons — graced the street corners of every town, and ubiquitous shrines in the city and countryside, as well as well-worn rosary beads used for simple prayers and desperate invocations, were as much a part of daily life as were food and clothing. Separating the faithful from Mary would be one of the hardest tasks the Reformers faced.

Accusations of Marian "worship" and the rejection of any Marian teaching that was not substantiated explicitly by Scripture served as the first Protestant wedge. The Protestant Reformers, however, failed to realize that in exalting the role of Mary as intercessor, and the lasting effects of her continuous fiat, the Church was raising up not only the Mother of God but all of womanhood as well. Catholic patrons knew that as Mary had been the conduit for the salvation of humanity, so she would remain a beacon to navigate the faithful through the stormy shoals of the Protestant Reformation.

The Catholic Restoration pressed this advantage, producing an astounding number of images of Mary, from humble maiden of Nazareth to glorious Queen of Heaven. She floats, flies, walks, offers, prays, embraces, protects—an astonishingly active figure, never merely a passive recipient of petitions, but ever engaged with the faithful. Artists grew in stature to become like teachers, sometimes illustrating the Marian doctrines that the Protestants rejected—such as the Immaculate Conception and the Assumption—other times using their creative skills to make delightful devotional images that would also impress theological truth upon their viewers.

The battle around intercession and indulgences grew increasingly acrimonious over the question of Purgatory. Denied almost universally by the Protestant Reformers, Purgatory had been one of the strongest links between the everyday faithful and the supernatural world, where those who died in "God's grace and friendship, but still imperfectly purified, are indeed assured of their eternal salvation." And after death "they undergo purification, so as to achieve the holiness necessary to enter the joy of heaven."[57] The connection between the living and dead through prayers and the liturgy formed a community that went beyond the saints venerated in the altarpieces to the souls of friends, loved ones, and even strangers who, through the Mystical Body of Christ, become part of the family of the faithful. The Church Militant (members of the Church on earth, striving against sin), the Church Suffering (the souls in Purgatory), and the Church Triumphant (the souls in Heaven) are parts of a whole and united Church. To remove one part destabilized the others in the hearts of the faithful.

Just as photography reminds people of friends and forges acquaintances among strangers, art served to create bonds between the living and the dead. Artists would imagine and illustrate another reality, showing brothers and sisters who had preceded them into the afterlife, a community waiting to be admitted into the presence of Christ.

Annibale, Agostino, and Ludovico Carracci (hereafter, the Carracci) painted weighty saints; Guido Reni, ethereal ones. A Bernini mystic floats in ecstasy while Caravaggio's martyr lies heavily on the ground. Pudgy putti frolic on the ceiling while warrior angels combat demons above altars. Artistic imaginations, limited only by requests for modesty and decorum, flourished, proposing a variety of images of men and women to serve as role models and inspiration. As the Church taught that the call to holiness was universal, artists showed that saints could come in every shape and size.

---

[57] *Catechism of the Catholic Church*, no. 1030.

Chapter 8

DIVINE MESSENGERS: ANGELS

St. John Paul II, standing at the threshold of the newly restored Sistine Chapel, was so moved by the images before him that he expressed his admiration in poetry, asking: "How make the invisible visible, how penetrate beyond the bounds of good and evil?"[58]

Before the glory of these freshly revealed frescoes, luminous after five hundred years of patina had been cleared away, John Paul articulated the amazement awakened by even the faintest glimpse of the divine. Michelangelo's hand had painted the frescoes, but his intellect had entered into the mystery of creation—not seen by human eyes. This endeavor to render visible the invisible would become a central theme of the Catholic Restoration, and the Church would expend tremendous efforts to highlight the constant, efficacious presence of grace despite the limitations of mortal vision.

This presence is nowhere more evident than in the activity of angels, spiritual beings who possess no material bodies and yet are integral to God's plan for the salvation of the world.

---

[58] Pope John Paul II, *Roman Triptych: Meditations*, trans. Jerzy Peterkiewicz (Vatican: Libreria Editrice Vaticana, 2003), 22.

While the Protestant Reformers never doubted the existence of angels—John Calvin duly noted that the Nicene Creed asserts the creation of things "visible and invisible," and Martin Luther offered some lovely reflections about angels—they sought to wean their followers off any sort of devotion to them.[59] Thus, the former Augustine monk also wrote, loosely alluding to St. Paul's letter to the Galatians, "So tenaciously should we cling to the world revealed by the Gospel, that were I to see all the Angels of Heaven coming down to tell me something different, not only would I not be tempted to doubt a single syllable, but I would shut my eyes and stop my ears for they would not deserve to be seen or heard."[60]

Among most of the Reformers, speculating about the angelic nature was discouraged. The fascination of the medieval Scholastics with invisible beings seemed like a waste of time to many Reformers. John Calvin wrote that "angels, being the ministers appointed to execute the commands of God, must, of course, be admitted to be his creatures, but to stir up questions concerning the time or order in which they were created, bespeaks more perverseness than industry."[61]

This position openly challenged St. Thomas Aquinas, known as the "Angelic Doctor," who had not only explained the sacrament of the Eucharist, but also categorized the nine orders of angels. Protestant authors critiqued the Scholastics' interest in what they thought were needless questions, creating the famous

---

[59] Calvin and Beveridge, *Institutes of the Christian Religion*, 147–149.

[60] Quoted in Eric Hoffer, *The True Believer: Thoughts on the Nature of Mass Movements* (New York: Harper and Row, 1951), 79.

[61] Calvin and Beveridge, *Institutes of the Christian Religion*, 144.

caricature of medieval theology as a school of friars pondering "whether a million angels may sit upon a needle's point."[62] But if the faithful never thought about angels, how could they invoke their aid against temptation and spiritual dangers?

Angels conferred a privileged role on artists in the Catholic Restoration as painters and sculptors enhanced the capacity of the visual arts to give form to ideas. As Protestant Reformer Ulrich Zwingli was moving toward the rejection of all images, Rome was encouraging artists to help the faithful see and meditate upon the invisible, especially the angels.

Angels proliferated in apses, vaults, holy-water stoups, and frescoes during the Catholic Restoration. Plump putti, armor-clad archangels, and lithe messengers emerged from stucco ceilings, frescoed clouds, plaster moldings, and marble cornices in unexpected ways. In teams or flying solo, a squadron of intercessors surrounded the faithful, always ready to accompany a soul or crush sin and temptation.

STAIRWAY TO HEAVEN

St. Peter's Basilica claims the title of the most ambitious project of the Catholic Restoration. With its soaring dome designed by Michelangelo, the church was completed in 1590 during the reign of Pope Sixtus V. Surmounting the tomb of St. Peter, where the successors of the Prince of the Apostles celebrate Mass, the commission for the interior decoration of the cupola was arguably the most prestigious of the era. The task fell to Giuseppe Cesari, Rome's most celebrated artist in the late 1580s, known by his honorific title: Cavaliere D'Arpino. The subject matter

---

[62] William Chillingworth, *The Religion of Protestants: A Safe Way to Salvation* (London: Henry Bohn, 1846), 12.

was most likely chosen by Cardinal Cesare Baronio, the church historian from Philip Neri's oratory in charge of organizing the decor of the new basilica.[63]

Cavaliere D'Arpino prepared the cartoons for the dome from 1603 to 1612. His drawings were simultaneously transposed into mosaic by the best mosaic artists of the period, working in the newly formed Vatican mosaic laboratory. The layout of the decoration was hierarchical and easy to read. Ninety-six figures, each enclosed in a contained space, rise in concentric circles toward the summit. The lowest row, barely noticeable in their tiny lunettes, depict the first sixteen canonized popes to be buried in the basilica. Above them, large full-length figures represent Jesus, Mary, St. Paul, and John the Baptist along with the twelve apostles: the founder of the Catholic Church and His earliest adherents seated in a circle around the tomb of Peter. Then the registers reveal angels, differentiated according to hierarchy of the Angelic Doctor. The embodied angels closest to the saints serve as messengers pointing upward or hold the instruments of Jesus' Passion to remind the faithful of Christ's salvific sacrifice. Reaching the Empyrean, the angels become more incorporeal, swathed in white robes as they assume attitudes of prayer or merely winged faces of infants absorbed wholly in loving contemplation of the Lord, much as a newborn looks toward his mother. A ring of blue flecked with golden stars frames a final burst of light from the lantern, where, at the apex of the dome, the viewer can make out the image of God the Father hovering

---

[63] Steven F. Ostrow, "Counter-Reformation and the End of the Century," in *Artistic Centers of the Italian Renaissance: Rome*, ed. Marcia Hall (New York: Cambridge University Press, 2003), 298.

Interior of the dome in St. Peter's Basilica by Giuseppe Cesari

above. Completely executed in shimmering golden mosaic tiles outlined in the blue of grace or the white of purity, the dome of St. Peter's dazzles but also firmly unites Heaven and earth through the ranks of angels.

THE GESÙ'S ARMY OF ANGELS

Old-school Scholastics formed an alliance with the newly founded Jesuits and Oratorians in defense of angels. The Jesuit church of the Gesù, built between 1568 and 1575, affirmed the importance of angels by emphasizing their role as mediators. St. Ignatius of Loyola wrote of angels and their active role in consolation and temptation in his *Spiritual Exercises*. In his view, visible or not, angels perceptibly affect the human soul. "The good Angel touches each soul sweetly, lightly, and gently, like a drop of water which enters into a sponge; and the evil one

Angeli che liberano le anime del Purgatorio by Federico Zuccari

touches it sharply and with noise and disquiet, as when the drop of water falls on a stone."[64]

To heighten awareness of the omnipresence of angels, the Jesuits dedicated a chapel in the Gesù to them. Ventura Salimbeni frescoed the vault with scriptural accounts of angels and their works: such as those associated with Tobias, Habakkuk, and Jacob in the Old Testament, ostensibly in agreement with the Protestant teachings. For the side walls, however, the Jesuits chose Federico Zuccari to encompass the viewer with images of angelic intercession: angels delivering souls from purgatory and angels bringing the prayers of the faithful to Heaven as invoked in the Eucharistic prayer.[65] Zuccari also painted the altarpiece,

---

[64] Ignatius of Loyola, *The Spiritual Exercises of St. Ignatius of Loyola*, trans. Elder Mullan, S.J. (New York: P.J. Kennedy and Sons, 1914), 231.

[65] The Roman Canon, confirmed by the Council of Trent, reads, "Almighty God, we pray that your angel may take this sacrifice to your altar in heaven."

Angeli che offrono a Dio le preghiere dei fedeli by Federico Zuccari

organizing his composition around the celestial hierarchy, with angels, archangels, and principalities; powers, virtues, and dominions; and finally, thrones, cherubim, and seraphim, those closest to the Holy Trinity. The entire chapel celebrates a hierarchy of intercession, where the angels play a fundamental role in mediating between God and man: a space filled with angelic activity, past and present, in the story of salvation.

THE RISE OF THE GUARDIAN ANGEL

The Jesuits had a particular affinity for angels. Robert Bellarmine thought long and hard about them; Francesco Albertini wrote something akin to a guidebook on them; and Aloysius Gonzaga's devotion to the guardian angels was legendary.[66] Little surprise,

---

[66] Francesco Albertini, *Trattato Dell'angelo Custode* (Rome: Bartolommeo Zannetti, 1612), was dedicated particularly to guardian angels, and Luigi Gonzaga was asked to pen a meditation on angels.

then, that the Society of Jesus would invite artists to develop the iconography of guardian angels.

Roman painter Domenico Fetti, who worked for the noble Gonzaga family that produced St. Aloysius, executed the haunting *Guardian Angel Protecting a Child from the Empire of the Devil* in 1618. Raised in Rome when Caravaggio burst on the scene, Fetti brought the tenebrist style with him to the Gonzaga court. In this work, a statuesque angel dominates the center of the canvas, his elegantly shod foot appearing to thrust into the viewer's space. The angel's face is kindly as he draws his prayerful ward into his safe embrace. The angel gestures toward Heaven, channeling a bright beam of light to the hopeful soul, whose hands are clasped in supplication. In the darkness, however, lurks a demon, flushed red with anger at being denied his prize. The angel's robe billows out like a shield, emphasizing the forceful arm he extends to keep sin at bay. Dozens of images like this proliferated in this era, constantly reminding the faithful that when assailed by temptation, angelic assistance was only a prayer away.

DEFEAT OF THE FALLEN ANGELS

St. Pius V (1566–1572), whose professed name was Michael after the archangel, took a marked interest in his namesake during his pontificate. He commissioned a little chapel to the warrior angel in the Vatican palace, which is now part of the museums and serves as a vestibule to the Sistine Chapel. In their rush to get inside, many visitors never look up to see Giorgio Vasari and Jacopo Zucchi's startling fresco of *The Fall of the Rebel Angels*.

In this work, seven exquisite angels in pastel armor pose gracefully while skewering seven misshapen demons. The wings of these disfigured creatures suggest that they were once angels, but through sin and defiance they have become a chaotic mishmash

*Guardian Angel Protecting a Child from the Empire
of the Demon* by Domenico Fetti

The Fall of the Rebel Angels by Giorgio Vasari and Jacopo Zucchi

of animal heads, tails, and claws grafted onto what were once beautiful bodies. A scorched cityscape encircles the base of the dome as buildings burn and crumble. The angels do not belong to the city of darkness but come from a ring of light in the center of the dome, where cherubs watch the ensuing combat.

This fresco served as more than an exercise in Scholastic theology. Pope Pius V excommunicated Britain's Queen Elizabeth for heresy, opposed the French Huguenots, gathered a fleet against the Ottoman Turks, and resisted internal pressures from Catholics who wanted to see the Church soften on doctrine in order to accommodate the new post-Reformation world. Pius responded to these challenges with the vigorous image of angels quelling rebellion, confident in serving the true Light.

Angels abound throughout the Eternal City, whether as childlike putti gamboling in stucco or elegant marble creatures accompanying pilgrims across the Ponte Sant'Angelo to St. Peter's Basilica. Their proliferation during the Catholic Restoration invited the faithful to engage the invisible with the mind, the senses, and especially the spirit.

Chapter 9

MARIA ADVOCATA NOSTRA

---❊---

The notion of Marian intercession posed quite a problem for Protestants. The rending of garments and gnashing of teeth over Marian doctrines such as the Assumption and the Immaculate Conception was far less troubling than dismissing centuries of images of the gentle Virgin comforting the faithful and directing prayers to her Son. Depictions of the Blessed Mother—from wide-eyed icons able to see the most intimate intentions, to images showing her capacious mantle gathering the faithful under her protection—had ingrained Mary in the Christian imagination as the "most gracious advocate," as she is called in the Salve Regina.

The Renaissance had transformed intercessory images of Mary into sacred conversations, where several saints, gathered around an enthroned Mother and Child, quietly invoked her for prayers and intentions. Symmetrical, harmonious, and tranquil, these works elegantly summed up centuries of accepted practice in prayer.

The Catholic Restoration reinvigorated images of Marian intercession, encouraging the faithful to turn to Mary with even more fervor in times of need. Mary became more active, seeking out the afflicted with energetic apparitions and gestures. The *Madonna of the Rosary*, the quintessential Marian devotion, was the first image to be renewed, thanks to artists such as Domenichino, Cigoli, Guido Reni, and Massimo Stanzione. In their works, the Blessed Mother was proactive, enthusiastically inviting the faithful to invoke her in prayer. The feast of the Holy Rosary had been established in 1573 shortly after the close of the Council of Trent, and, in its wake, these depictions abounded in religious houses, in churches, and even in private homes.

A Light in the Darkness

Perhaps the most striking was Caravaggio's version, painted in 1607. The powerful Colonna family, whose armorial device, a column, holds the composition together, probably commissioned the work to celebrate Marcantonio Colonna's having commanded the papal fleet to victory at the Battle of Lepanto on October 7, 1571, the date that would become first the feast of Our Lady of Victory and then the feast of the Holy Rosary.

Caravaggio rejected the traditional iconography of depicting the Blessed Virgin floating on heavenly clouds and supported by cushions of angels, choosing instead to seat Mary in a crowded room, only slightly elevated above the throng. A few Dominican saints gather around her, a common compositional practice, given that St. Dominic is credited with having promoted the practice of the Rosary. St. Peter Martyr, recognizable by the gash left by an axe in his forehead, turns to the viewers, encouraging them to join the petitioners. A mother and child kneel alongside a barefoot beggar and a noble in discreet finery (probably the patron), all beseeching Mary's intercession. Caravaggio's stark figures, rigorously drawn from life, lend an immediacy to

Madonna of the Rosary by Caravaggio

the scene: all kinds of people require heavenly assistance, and the Mother of God hears everyone's prayers.

Caravaggio chose to stretch a scarlet curtain as a backdrop, as opposed to filling the space with the cerulean clouds favored by his rivals, the Carracci. Red, the color of mortality, sets the stage of human needs and fears that drive the faithful to Our Lady. A mysterious light enters from the right, caressing her face but focused on the nude child in her arms, Jesus, who looks out at the viewer. Mary fixes her gaze on St. Dominic, her foreshortened hand thrust forward to direct the saint to distribute the rosaries. Caravaggio does not deny the direct communication between the faithful and Christ, but he also acknowledges that one might want to gain the support of His Mother.

MOTHER OF ALL

Barocci was the stylistic antithesis of Caravaggio, with his over-flowing compositions, brilliant colors, and lovely figures, but the two were often commissioned for the same sites. Together they offered a great breadth of vision, especially as regards the Virgin Mary. Caravaggio's twelve figures in the *Madonna of the Rosary* seem like a paltry turnout when compared with the more than three dozen men, women, children, and even a dog packing Barocci's *Madonna del Popolo*, painted for the Confraternity of Santa Maria della Misericordia in Arezzo in 1578. Confraternities were associations of pious laymen committed to doing charitable acts of mercy, including everything from almsgiving to the burial of the dead. The brothers, to affirm Mary's intercessory role, requested that the painter produce "the mystery of the misericordia or some other mystery and histories of the most glorious Virgin," but Barocci demurred, thinking himself more suited to events such as the Assumption or the

Visitation.[67] Ultimately both parties agreed on the image of Maria Mediatrix, interceding on behalf of the people with her Son. This Franciscan conception of Mary as Mediatrix seems to have been suggested by the painter, whose close affiliation with the order was such that he remembered them in his will.[68]

Barocci always favored the symmetrical compositional shape of the triangle, yet in this work he threw the symmetry slightly off balance. The dove of the Holy Spirit anchors the center of the work, but Jesus, floating in the heavens, is pushed slightly to the left to make room for His Mother. The Virgin, suspended only slightly below, approaches her Son on behalf of the *popolo* — the people. The image of Mary flanking Jesus, instead of below Him, or, in rarer cases, alone with her outstretched mantle, defined the iconography of the Maria Mediatrix and had been used to powerful effect by Michelangelo in his *Last Judgment* painting in 1541. As a young man, Barocci had met the great Florentine master in Rome, where he received praise for his drawings. Barocci's admiration was such that he would often employ Michelangelo's foreshortening technique of thrusting figures toward the viewer, whether in his *Institution of the Eucharist* or in this work, where the toddler's bare foot faces the viewer and draws attention through the charm of the child.

Underneath, a torrent of humanity flows in living color. Nobles kneel alongside beggars, and children frolic amid the disabled in a glorious sea of light and color. The people assist one another: giving alms, distributing food, visiting the

---

[67] Nicholas Turner, *Federico Barocci*, authorized English-language ed. (Paris: Société Nouvelle Adam Biro, 2000), 69.

[68] Keith Christiansen, "Barocci, the Franciscans, and a Possible Funerary Gift," *Burlington Magazine* 147 (2005): 722–728.

Madonna del Popolo by Federico Barocci

imprisoned—the corporal works of mercy on earth reflect Mary's request for mercy in Heaven.

Barocci shared with Caravaggio an eye for fine detail. The sparkling jewels, the finely woven basket, and the wooden instrument root the activity on earth, but the luminous color and upward composition evoke the Lord's kingdom, "on earth as it is in Heaven."

MARY WANTS YOU

Thirty-year-old Ludovico Carracci revolutionized the iconography of the sacred conversation with his *Bargellini Madonna*, painted in 1588 for the Carmelite Church of Sts. John and Philip in Bologna. The altarpiece was destined for the chapel of the influential Bargellini clan in a convent for Convertite, women who had abandoned a life of prostitution to take religious vows. Ludovico exchanged the equilateral triangle favored by Renaissance compositions for the strong diagonal of the isosceles, directing the gaze more emphatically to his intended focal point.

Mary is enthroned high on the right-hand side of the painting, drawing the viewer's eye off-center. Directly below her, wearing bright robes in hues of scarlet and pumpkin, is Mary Magdalene, offering her precious vial of oil. On the left, St. Dominic and St. Francis don humble habits in more subdued colors. Between the two, a member of the Bargellini family kneels, swathed in her widow's veil. Ludovico renders the luminous effects of silks and silver around Mary and the Magdalene but then employs dark, earthy colors for the mendicant saints. The Bargellini widow, born into privilege, has offered her beautiful things to Christ and cloaks herself in simple, somber robes.

Frenetic activity fills the gap between the saints and the Virgin and Child. Angels tumble from the heavens with incense and

Bargellini Madonna by Ludovico Carracci

crowns, Dominic extends his hands toward the Virgin, Francis presents the pious widow to the Holy Family, and Mary Magdalene reaches up to offer her gift. The viewer, however, is not excluded from this activity. The sharp foreshortening places the beholder underneath, gazing up at the saintly assembly while noting the two distinctive towers of Bologna receding in the distance; yet Mary, from her high perch, turns to look down directly at the beholder. Simultaneously, Mary Magdalene's free hand gestures toward the viewer, who would have been the converted prostitutes who frequented the church. A gap at the base of the composition seems to await the visitor, an open invitation to join the holy congregation. Thus, these women, who had left the worldly life of the city, found more loving company in the house of the Virgin.

Ludovico's painting was groundbreaking for more than its composition. Five years after Archbishop Gabriele Paleotti had published the *Discourse on Sacred and Profane Images* in Bologna, urging painters to communicate more effectively and "to struggle as hard as they can to win the mind of every viewer,"[69] Ludovico, a native of the same city, produced a work that engaged the faithful in a new way.

By opening a gap for the beholder, Ludovico designated a path in the painting, with Mary as the guiding star, leading toward the goal of Christ. This active viewer engagement would develop into the theatrical style of Baroque art.

---

[69] Paleotti, *Discourse on Sacred and Profane Images*, 310.

Chapter 10

MARY AS TEACHER

———————————————— ❊ ————————————————

The Protestant Reformers never questioned the Virgin Mary's title of "Theotokos" or "God-Bearer," as decreed at the Council of Ephesus in 431. Alongside the Virgin Birth, Marian teachings borne out by Scripture were uncontested. Martin Luther admired the Virgin as the "highest woman and the noblest gem in Christianity after Christ. . . . She is nobility, wisdom, and holiness personified."[70]

The Reformers, however, tended to view Mary's role as a passive one. They viewed her as a vessel, made to receive God and then to be placed on a shelf for admiration and emulation, whereas the Catholics saw Mary as constantly active on our behalf. In Catholic teaching, her fiat had grown beyond a submissive yielding to the divine will into an active trust in and cooperation with God and intercession for others. In developing her thought regarding the Blessed Virgin Mary, the Roman Church anchored her life in two supernatural events: her Immaculate Conception—being conceived in the womb of her mother without the

---

[70] *The Complete Sermons of Martin Luther*, vol. 7 (Grand Rapids, MI: Baker Books, 2000), 209–220.

stain of original sin—and her bodily Assumption into Heaven. These teachings were not explicitly found in Scripture, and therefore were suspect for Protestants.

Although only recently defined as dogmas (the Immaculate Conception in 1854 and the Assumption in 1950), these devotions had existed for centuries, having developed through the years from the earliest teachings of the Church. Sts. Ambrose and Augustine had discoursed extensively about the sinlessness of Mary and her spotlessness as the vessel of the Incarnation.[71]

During the Renaissance, Pope Sixtus IV included the Immaculate Conception on December 8 in the liturgical calendar. This profoundly Marian pope went on to dedicate his Sistine Chapel to her Assumption. In this era, Marian imagery was evolving away from icons and into the more action-packed world of Renaissance narrative. Following the example of the earliest Church Fathers, Mary was often compared with Eve, whose sinful action had helped bring about the Fall. Conversely, Mary, through her active obedience, would help bring about Redemption.

Although the Immaculate Conception reflected Mary as a heroic figure prepared at the beginning of time for her tremendous undertaking, art struggled to keep up with this heady, nonnarrative concept, employing the likes of Leonardo da Vinci to delve into this complex theology in his *Virgin of the Rocks*. Michelangelo even took a crack at the subject in the Sistine Chapel. By placing the *Creation of Woman* as the central panel

---

[71] "Mary, a Virgin not only undefiled but a Virgin whom grace has made inviolate, free of every stain of sin." Ambrose, Sermon 22, 30.

of the ceiling, he underscored Mary's role as the New Eve, a theological notion dating back to early Christianity that was given its finest modern consolidated expression three hundred years later by Blessed John Henry Newman.[72]

This expanded role of Mary had taken deep root among the faithful. It conferred a special dignity on all women and gave this exceptional Mother extraordinary powers to intercede in the lives of the devout. For the pious populace, denial of this beloved tradition was painful and simply unacceptable.

With no official teaching however, it was hard to refute Melanchthon's view that the Immaculate Conception was "an invention of monks,"[73] and when Calvin mocked the idea, writing that "as to the special privilege of the Virgin Mary, when they produce the celestial diploma we shall believe what they say," how were the faithful to respond?

Marian doctrine became one of the most exciting ateliers for artists, and as they wrestled with the ancient writings and concepts that the Immaculate Conception and the Assumption implied, painters reached the most prestigious heights of their field, becoming, as Gabriele Paleotti had once exhorted, "tacit preachers to the people."[74] Spurred by this ecclesiastical display of trust, the painters of the Catholic Restoration would ultimately create the definitive iconography of the Immaculate Conception.

---

[72] John Henry Newman, *The Second Eve* (Charlotte, NC: Tan Books, 1991), 9–13.
[73] Remigius Bäumer, "Reformation," in *Marienlexikon* (St. Ottilien: EOS Verlag, 1992), 424.
[74] Paleotti, *Discourse on Sacred and Profane Images*, 310.

A WOMAN CLOTHED WITH THE SUN

The Carracci school was the artistic academy most attuned to the ideas of the Catholic Restoration, having been formed during the tenure of Archbishop Paleotti. It was the restless, imaginative Ludovico who first endeavored to illustrate Mary of the Immaculate Conception in 1590 in the painting known as the *Madonna dei Scalzi* for the Discalced Carmelites of Bologna, founded by St. Teresa of Avila and St. John of the Cross twenty years earlier.

Ludovico paints Mary suspended in midair—an iconographic device invented by Raphael in his *Sistine Madonna* in nearby Piacenza. This holy levitation would become the standard in images of both the Immaculate Conception and the Assumption. Mary, encircled by stars, stands on a crescent moon evoking the woman of the apocalypse in Revelation: "A great portent appeared in heaven, a woman clothed with the sun, with the moon under her feet, and on her head a crown of twelve stars" (Rev. 12:1).

Tempering his novelty, Ludovico depicted Mary with the infant Christ in her arms, maintaining the more traditional Madonna and Child iconography, so as not to shock the public, and also emphasizing the centrality of Christ, so as to avoid the Protestant accusation that Catholics held Mary in greater esteem than Jesus.

The two saints standing by her side reaffirm the continuous tradition of the Immaculate Conception: St. Francis, founder of the order that tirelessly promoted the Immaculate Conception, and St. Jerome, who succinctly affirmed, "Death by Eve, life by Mary" back in the fourth century.[75]

---

[75] St. Jerome, "Epistle 22: To Eustochium," http://www.newadvent.org/fathers/3001022.htm.

Madonna dei Scalzi by Ludovico Carracci

PURE AND IMMACULATE

Ludovico's work was continued by one of his finest students, Guido Reni. Reni produced a great many images of both of these Marian doctrines, but perhaps his most beautiful effort was his *Immaculate Conception*, painted in 1626 for King Philip IV of Spain. Reni omitted saints, Church Doctors, and the Christ Child, leaving Mary to float on a crescent moon supported by a trio of angels. More cherubs surround her as she gazes raptly toward the heavens. Her clothes retain the traditional red and blue, red symbolizing the mortal woman cloaked in the blue robe of grace, but the golden light that suffuses her alludes to the abundant favor bestowed upon her.

Bartolomé Esteban Murillo was a mere boy when Reni's painting arrived in Madrid, bastion of the Immaculate Conception. This belief was so strongly held in the city that when, in 1613, an itinerant preacher argued against the devotion, forty thousand citizens took to the streets to reclaim this singular honor of Mary.[76] Murillo painted the subject repeatedly and, in 1678, created the image of the Immaculate Conception best known today, which was later validated by Mary's miraculous apparition at Rue du Bac in Paris. Mary, seen as youthful maiden untouched by age, now wears white, symbol of her unblemished purity, under her blue mantle. The angels below offer up symbols of her glory. With Mary's perfect purity (the lily), and with our prayers (the roses for the Rosary), she helps us to persevere to victory (the palm) and eternal peace (the olive).

---

[76] Enriqueta Harris, *Complete Studies on Velázquez* (Madrid: Centro de Estudios Europa Hispánica, 2006), 259.

The Immaculate Conception by Guido Reni

The Immaculate Conception by Bartolomé Esteban Perez Murillo

FROM DORMITION TO ASSUMPTION

Artists worked no less tirelessly on the Assumption than on the Immaculate Conception. An ancient teaching, the Assumption held that Mary knew no corporeal decay but entered Heaven together with her body. The lack of veneration of any bodily relics of Mary or a tradition of her resting place underscored the antiquity of this belief. The earliest version of the feast, the Dormition of the Virgin, was often illustrated by a sleeping Mary with Jesus holding a miniature version of the Virgin in His arms. A frequently depicted epilogue showed Mary crowned in Heaven by her Son, but in the Renaissance the Assumption began to appear discreetly, usually representing Mary as a weightless sylph floating upward amid musical angels.

The artists of the Catholic Restoration were invited to think more deeply about the meaning of the Assumption and, in doing so, came up with a fascinating variety of thought-provoking images for the subject.

ASLEEP IN CHRIST

In 1605, Caravaggio painted an image of the Dormition of the Virgin for the Discalced Carmelites of Rome. He chose to show the lifeless body of Mary surrounded by sorrowful apostles, intended to leave the viewer anxiously awaiting something more to happen. The commission had asked for the scene of Mary's death, and Caravaggio complied by stretching a heavy, middle-aged body sprawled and lifeless on her deathbed. Her feet bared and ankles exposed, Mary is wrapped in a red dress, symbolic of her mortality. Her blue robe of grace has dimmed to gray. The eye is led down toward Mary Magdalene and then further down toward the ground, where she should soon be buried. But in the upper left, unseen by the group lost in grief, a light enters the

The Death of the Virgin by Caravaggio

room, drawing attention to the red curtain covering the upper part of the painting. This is only the end of the act, not the end of the play. That light, supernatural in nature—as there is neither window nor lantern to produce it—promises that out of the darkness of this moment will come one of the most beautiful miracles in history, the Assumption. One must have faith … and patience.

MARY RISES

The Carmelites, as it happens, had no patience with Caravaggio's version of the scene and rejected the work. To replace it, they hired a less provocative artist, Carlo Saraceni, to repeat the commission. He showed the Dormition with the apostles standing around Mary's deathbed but eschewed the depiction of her lifeless body in favor of a Mary sitting up under the opening heavens, conflating the Dormition and the Assumption into a less challenging scene.

Caravaggio was probably reacting to Annibale Carracci, who had become the undisputed Roman master of the *Assumption* with his painting in Santa Maria del Popolo. The altarpiece of the Cerasi Chapel (where Caravaggio had painted *The Death of Peter* and *The Conversion of Saul*), Carracci's painting had greeted the pilgrims during the Jubilee Year 1600 with a vivid reminder of the importance of Mary in the life of the Church.

Annibale's Mary is no waif-like creature, but a voluminous woman floating upward. Her face radiant, Mary rises above the cavernous darkness of the tomb toward the golden light of heaven above. Her dainty, bare foot points toward the viewer as if she might fly overhead while the astonished apostles look on in awe. The buoyant colors and the compressed composition underscore the glorious nature of this mystery. Caravaggio, on the other hand, ponders the fearful moment before the miracle.

The Death of the Virgin by Carlo Saraceni

Assumption of the Virgin by Annibale Carracci

As the most depicted woman in human history, Mary offered artists opportunities to expand their creative capabilities. Accompanying the Church in her developing teaching on Mary, art created proportionately fascinating images of the Queen of Heaven.

Chapter 11

THE TWIN REFOUNDERS
OF CHRISTIAN ROME

❖

The extraordinary beauty that accompanies visitors to Rome from one end of the Eternal City to the other is, in large part, due to a Galilean fisherman named Simon, now better known to us as St. Peter. The death of the Prince of the Apostles at the hands of Emperor Nero around 64 determined that Rome would be the enduring seat of the Christian Church. The conclave elects the Bishop of Rome, and as successor to St. Peter, the pope is entrusted with the solemn duty of conserving and transmitting the deposit of faith.

The legacy of Peter has seen plenty of upsets over the centuries—temporal threats from secular princes, invasions by Saracens, and even the seventy-year exodus of the papal court to Avignon in France—but the Protestant Reformation brought an entirely different challenge to the Petrine succession. It claimed that the papacy had no importance at all in the life of the faithful. The annihilation of the papacy, in fact, was absolutely central to the Reformers' self-appointed task of refounding the Church.

Martin Luther began by denying that the authority of the pope derived from Christ's statement to Peter: "You are Peter, and on this rock I will build my church, and the powers of death shall not prevail against it" (Matt. 16:18), claiming instead that the papacy is a human institution created by men—or worse. By 1545, Luther was writing "Against the Papacy at Rome, an Institution of the Devil," in which he railed against the Roman pontiff, saying, in one of his milder invectives, it is "very easy to prove that the pope is neither the commander or head of Christendom, nor lord of the world above emperor, councils, and everything, as he lies, blasphemes, curses, and raves in his decretals, to which the hellish Satan drives him."[77]

Luther's friend Lucas Cranach produced a series of Illustrations of the pope as the Antichrist that have gone down in history as the first, and maybe harshest, of papal satires. The Protestants had struck at the heart of Petrine supremacy theologically, scripturally, historically, and artistically.

The problem was aggravated by the Reformers' co-opting of St. Paul as the principal apostolic authority. Roman tradition had always seen Peter and Paul as "brothers": dying on the same day, June 29, they were born simultaneously in Heaven, and like the twins Romulus and Remus, founders of ancient Rome, the two saints became the twin founders of Christian Rome. A millennium of images showing their respective martyrdoms, as well as the joint feast day, commemorated the brotherly bond between the two. The Protestants broke that bond.

MICHELANGELO TO THE RESCUE

On the artistic front, the Church fought fire with fire, unleashing the towering inferno of Michelangelo against Cranach's spindly

---

[77] "Against the Roman Papacy, an Institution of the Devil" in *Luther's Works on CD-ROM*, vol. 41, 341.

engravings. Fresh from his first Protestant response in *The Last Judgment*, the sixty-eight-year-old Florentine artist was given two more prestigious commissions. The first was to complete the magnificent basilica dedicated to St. Peter, marking the tomb of the Prince of the Apostles, and the second was to paint the Pauline Chapel. Cranach and his woodcuts never stood a chance.

The Pauline Chapel was built for the pope's personal Masses, adoration of the Blessed Sacrament, and the conclave. The most Roman Catholic of spaces, it underscored mystery, martyrdom, and magisterium. Michelangelo frescoed the side walls from 1542 to 1550 with an unusual pairing of pictures — the right wall showed *The Crucifixion of St. Peter*, not surprising given the proximity of his tomb, but the left wall illustrated *The Conversion of Saul*. This new combination, requested by the pope, reiterated the significance of Peter's ultimate witness, which took place a stone's throw from the chapel, but was now complemented with Saul's encounter with truth. This image served as a reprimand to Protestant sympathizers, a summons to turn from the wrong road and return to the light and to the Church that Jesus had founded.

Recent cleaning completed in 2009 has revealed that Michelangelo, despite age and eye trouble, had lost none of his artistic power. Most art historians had dismissed this work as the unfortunate expression of a man whose faculties were failing, but instead, the colors are mesmerizing, the composition fascinating, and the message authoritative. In *The Crucifixion of St. Peter*, people swirl in turbulent eddies around the dominant figure of the apostle. Michelangelo, for the first time since his youth, displayed a dazzling palette of lapis, mulberry, mustard, cranberry, and olive in the crowd, highlighting Peter. Forcefully illuminated in the nude, except for a loincloth, he bears witness to the naked truth.

The Crucifixion of St. Peter by Michelangelo Buonarroti

Helpless women weep, curious onlookers approach, soldiers bustle, and men converse, but Peter, stretched on his cross, remains indifferent to the drama around him. He lifts his head to stare directly at the viewer, which, in the case of the conclaves held in the chapel, was potentially a future pope. Michelangelo's St. Peter reminds his successors of the real papal job description: unflagging witness, no matter the immediate situations, dangers, and dramas. Peter's fierce gaze then follows the newly elected pope from the altar and out the door, a daunting example.

Across from the painting of Peter, in *The Conversion of Saul*, Saul lies stunned on the ground. Blinded, he holds his hand above

The Conversion of Saul by Michelangelo Buonarroti

his eyes as he struggles to rise. The intensity of this encounter has an effect similar to that of a missile hitting its target: most figures run away in fear while the remainder cower before the heavenly manifestation. Christ, spectacularly foreshortened so as to appear to fly down toward Saul, emits a ray of dazzling light that cuts through clouds and crowds to find its mark. Christ's other hand gestures forcefully toward the distance, indicating to Saul to get up and go. As the viewer walks by, he is first confronted with the shock of Saul's realization of his errors and then follows Christ's hand to see a city in the distance—conversion is good, but conversion and witness is better.

FOLLOW-UP BY CARAVAGGIO

Fifty years after the completion of the Pauline chapel, Pope Clement VIII wanted to repeat this Petrine emphasis for the Jubilee Year 1600, and he turned to his treasurer, Tiberio Cerasi, who commissioned a chapel in the church of Santa Maria del Popolo. This church, the first one pilgrims would see upon their entry into Rome through the northern gate, had a special significance in the Catholic Restoration. This church was run by Augustinians, the order of Martin Luther, who as a young monk had preached here ninety years earlier. To exorcise this memory, Cerasi chose the painter Caravaggio, catapulted to fame a year earlier with his *St. Matthew* series in San Luigi dei Francesi.

For his second public work, Caravaggio (whose real name was Michelangelo Merisi) was competing with the legacy of his Florentine namesake, who had died seven years before he was born. The subjects would be the same, *The Martyrdom of Peter* and *The Conversion of Saul*, but where Michelangelo had covered great expanses with fresco, Caravaggio had one-third the space and was working in the less prestigious medium of oil, which had been derided by the older master as suitable for women and lazy artists. Furthermore, his archrival, Annibale Carracci, had already been awarded the *Assumption* altarpiece, so the bright colors and virtuoso foreshortening of the Bolognese painter would vie for the viewer's attention.

Caravaggio dared to redesign the images entirely. Whereas Michelangelo painted crowds, Caravaggio painted intimate seclusion; whereas Michelangelo had cobalt skies, Caravaggio painted encroaching darkness.

His *Crucifixion of St. Peter* features four figures versus Michelangelo's fifty. All four are hard at work; three are laboring to complete the execution, while Peter's task is to stay the distance and

The Crucifixion of St. Peter by Caravaggio

remain on the cross. The three executioners have been reduced to muscle groups, a red deltoid, a yellow gluteus, and a green trapezius all flexing like cogs in a machine. Their faces remain in darkness; they are unknown and unknowing. They could be anyone, in ignorance, blindly working to destroy the Faith. Peter, however, is bathed in a light so powerful that it beautifies his bulky body and reveals his full knowledge of his mission. He gazes at the nail in his hand as if to grasp it even tighter, for through this trial he will receive the greatest reward.

A large stone lies in the foreground, a play on Peter's name, which means "rock." After a long journey, the pilgrims can take heart; only a few more steps to the place where the rock was laid to rest. The reality of St. Peter—his death in Rome, his body under the high altar of the newly completed Vatican basilica—would be made present to them through the stark painting of Caravaggio, along with the reminder that St. Peter did not die for the teachings of Luther, but those of Christ, whom he knew and followed to his brutal death in Nero's arena.

The Conversion on the Way to Damascus emphasized the intimacy of conversion. Here, Caravaggio further reduced the number of figures to only three. The canvas is almost entirely occupied by a heavy workhorse and its handler, pausing as Saul lies on the ground. The inverted-gymnast Jesus of Michelangelo is gone, and all that is left is His light, which, unnoticed by the animal or its master, beams down upon Saul alone. Saul's spiritual awakening is personal, and he receives it open-armed. Caravaggio uses minimalist tones of brown and beige in most of the space, until he reaches Saul. There the palette ignites as the red cloak spread below him and the orange cuirass evoke the colors of fire. Caravaggio's hues illustrate the kindling of the Holy Spirit as Saul begins his transformation into Paul, Apostle to the Gentiles.

Caravaggio did absorb one important lesson from Michelangelo as he worked on his canvases. Michelangelo's Pauline compositions focused downward in both frescoes, leading the

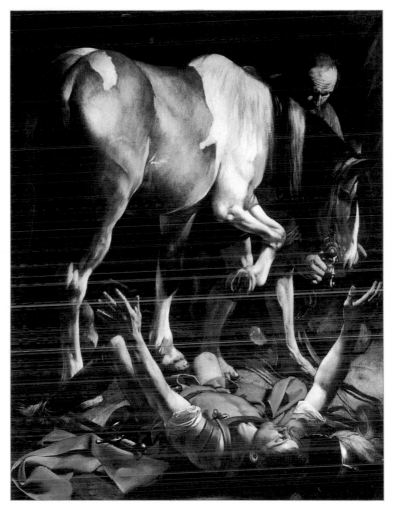

The Conversion on the Way to Damascus by Caravaggio

eye through the jumble of characters to the heroes placed at the lower edge of the work. Traditionally, art tended to lift the eye upward in compositions, but Michelangelo's inverted V shape challenged that.

Caravaggio would take it much further in his art, stressing prostrate protagonists at the bottom of his canvases. This humble position, prone and vulnerable, became a favorite of the artist, reminding the faithful, who would often have to bend down to follow his compositions, that humility is the key to sanctity. Peter and Paul accepted the humiliations of sin, error, derision, and persecution, but emerged purified and powerful, ready to navigate the fledgling Church into her great journey through centuries, continued by the unbroken line of Peter's successors.

Chapter 12

MYSTIC UNION

❧

Catholic mystics garnered the maximum skepticism from Protestant Reformers. The ecstasies claimed by the saints where they experienced soaring visions of divine union elicited mostly eye rolling and derision. The Protestants certainly didn't eschew closeness to Christ through prayer—John Calvin even drew from St. Bernard of Clairvaux when developing his ideas of "election" with its deep, personal, certitude of salvation—but they recoiled at the "excesses" of the Catholic Church.[78] The Protestants saw mystical experience as a quiet, peaceful assurance, while the Catholics had a greater flair for the dramatic.

Catholic mysticism was deeply rooted, passionate, and often described in physical or even sensual terms. Literature, art, and music tended to portray ecstatic transport as intense and fleeting, an overwhelming foretaste of the joy that awaits in Heaven. Medieval scholars defined mystical theology as "the experiential knowledge of God through the union of spiritual affection with

---

[78] Stanford W. Reid, "Bernard of Clairvaux in the Thought of John Calvin," *Westminster Theological Journal* 41, no. 1 (1978).

Him."[79] This "affection," or perhaps this more naked realization of God's love, left at times more than just spiritual or intellectual awareness; it also left physical marks, such as the stigmata, in the case of St. Francis of Assisi and others. The body, made in the image and likeness of God, and assumed by God-made-Man, shared the experience of divine love with the soul, at which point the Catholics and the Protestants parted ways.

As Protestants increasingly subsumed knowledge of God into the intellectual sphere, Catholic art strove to manifest the experiential, even the sensual, nature of oneness with the Lord. Art was especially equipped to be of service for this challenge, since it was already expected to excite piety by stimulating the sense of sight.

After the Reformation, the Catholic Church increased her commemoration of mystics, both on the altars and in art. Thanks to the finest painters, the visions of newly canonized Mary Maddelena de' Pazzi, Aloysius Gonzaga, and the rapt St. Ignatius became a common sight in chapels. Even older saints with more established iconographies found a new attitude, reminding the faithful that long before the Reformation, holy men and women had basked in the Lord's consuming love.

St. Francis: From Tree Hugger to Mystic

One of the more drastic makeovers of a familiar beloved saint was that of St. Francis of Assisi. Portrayals of the Franciscan founder changed dramatically from the tree-hugging, wolf-taming, bird-preaching saint to the ecstatic recipient of the Lord's wounds on his own body, the stigmata. Many artists, from Carracci to Caravaggio,

---

[79] Jean Gerson and André Combes, *De Mystica Theologia*, Theasaurus Mundi Bibliotheca Scriptorum Latinorum Mediae et Recentioris Aetatis (Rome: In Aedibus Theasure Mundi, 1968), 65.

represented Francis in this transported state, but Barocci's *St. Francis* has an unexpected and arresting power. Close to the Capuchin Order (indeed buried in their church in Urbino), Barocci had a personal devotion to St. Francis that permeates this work. Cramped in a tight, almost tomb-like cave, Francis stands at the narrow passageway between the viewer and the mysterious expanse beyond. In the distance, dawn is breaking, the hour when, according

St. Francis by Federico Barocci

to biographies of the saint, he received the stigmata. St. Francis has started his prayer with Scripture — the Bible lies open before him — but he has turned his mind and heart toward the crucified Christ before him. Here the dull grays and browns of mortality recede as Francis gazes at the crucifix, shining with inner energy. Eyes glistening, the saint shares an intimacy with the suffering Christ that transforms the cross from an inanimate object to a modeled body leaning toward the open-armed Francis. It is intimate, intense, and real. The passion of the saint's prayer has evoked an experience from the Word of God to the presence of God. Francis's foreshortened hand projects toward the viewer, ready to penetrate out from the confines of the canvas. The hard iron stud in his hand glints close to the beholder, taking this vision out of the realm of mere intellectual fascination into empirical reality.

ST. PHILIP NERI: LEVITY AND LEVITATION

St. Philip Neri offered artists an irresistible combination of shrewd practicality, jolly humor, and intense visionary experience. One day St. Philip would tell a young man to wear a fox tail as a penance to curb his vanity; the next he would allow dogs into church to tame their lazy owners; and then he would levitate before the altar, absorbed in the love of Christ's presence.

In 1721, painter Marco Benefial captured all the amazement of the supernatural erupting into the everyday in his *Vision of St. Philip Neri*. As a fair-haired child pulls away in fear, exclaiming, "Look! That man is possessed by the devil!" her mother rebukes her: "That man is a saint and he is in ecstasy."[80] Benefial pulled

---

[80] Pietro Giacomo Bacci, *The Life of Saint Philip Neri: Apostle of Rome and Founder of the Congregation of the Oratory*, 2nd ed. (London: Paternoster House, 1902), 343.

The Vision of St. Philip Neri by Marco Benefial

Philip Neri's ecstatic state out of the shadows and into the open by including witnesses and bystanders. Many people had seen the saint transported and were converted by the sight, but that little girl closest to the viewer makes one wonder what his own reaction would be in the presence of such an overt and personal display of divine love.

Benefial calls the senses into play by painting musical instruments to recall the sound of the music, lilies to evoke the scent of flowers, and the chalice stimulating the sense of taste. The musical instruments also served as a reminder of the Oratory founded by Philip, where sacred dramas would be set to music. The beauty of both music and painting were called into service by this saint, whose own life was a colorful canvas of holiness, humor, and humility.

The physical elevation of the saint takes place as he consecrates the Host. Benefial intertwines the natural world and the divine in a moment of ravishing beauty — not to be feared or distrusted but devoutly to be desired. Art allows us to live, albeit distantly, this extraordinary encounter.

St. Teresa: An Education in Ecstasy

Gian Lorenzo Bernini stood on the shoulders of the brilliant artists of the Catholic Restoration to proclaim the triumphant era of the Baroque. Born well after the close of Trent, the Florentine sculptor crafted the image of mysticism that would be more disturbing to Protestants than any other: the *Ecstasy of St. Teresa.* Begun twenty years after Teresa of Avila's canonization, this work combined painting, sculpture, and architecture to re-create the saint's well-documented experience of ecstasy. Situated in the Cornaro Chapel in Santa Maria della Vittoria (built to celebrate a 1618 Catholic victory over Protestant forces at the Battle of White Mountain), the space is veneered in red jasper, evoking the world of the flesh. While sculpted portraits of the Cornaro family occupy the lateral galleries, the viewer stands at center stage as the red gives way to a large niche bathed in light, reminiscent of a proscenium in a theater. There, Teresa is suspended, like a special effect in a modern movie, reclining on a cloud as an angel lifts her robe, flaming dart in hand. In the words of the saint herself, he was:

> thrusting it at times into my heart, and to pierce my very entrails; when he drew it out, he seemed to draw them out also, and to leave me all on fire with a great love of God. The pain was so great, that it made me moan; and yet so surpassing was the sweetness of this excessive pain, that I could not wish to be rid of it. The soul is satisfied now with nothing less than God. The pain is not bodily, but spiritual; though the body has its share in it.[81]

Natural light bathes the sacred scene from a hidden window above the group: Bernini has transposed Caravaggio's effect of light from a mysterious source to the medium of architecture. Above, on the high vault, he frescoed a dove hovering amid clouds. This experience, deeply personal yet revealed in the Spanish saint's writings, becomes visible to viewers thanks to Bernini's creativity. This devoutly faithful sculptor had grown up at the cosmopolitan court of Pope Paul V, where Galileo arrived to demonstrate his telescope. As science gave man a way to see the invisible bodies of nature, so Bernini became the means through which man could see the invisible movements of the spirit.

---

[81] *The Life of St. Teresa of Jesus, of the Order of Our Lady of Carmel*, trans. David Lewis, 3rd ed. (London: T. Baker, 1904), 255–256.

The Ecstasy of St. Teresa by Gian Lorenzo Bernini

The work was so compelling, and such a powerful argument for the Catholic experience of divine love, that Enlightenment detractors saw fit to undermine it, from critiquing Bernini's skill to suggesting that the work carried another, more profane meaning. Later centuries seemed so distanced from the concept of divine love that they could see only a very earthly form of desire in the work. Whether the sophisticated "nudge, nudge, wink, wink" of a French dignitary de Brosse or the disingenuous marveling of a Stendhal at "clever Bernini"[82] for sneaking an erotic scene into a church, the uplifting illustration of divine union has been whittled away to Dan Brown's absurd observation in *Angels and Demons:* "Pope Urban VIII had rejected *The Ecstasy of St. Teresa* as too sexually explicit for the Vatican."[83]

Ex stasis — the experience of being taken outside oneself — previews Heaven, where the resurrected body together with the soul will be united with God, and all the efforts and labors of holiness will be rewarded. Teresa's face, emulating that of Christ in Michelangelo's *Pietà*, is the ultimate image of total self-offering to God, as well as the knowledge, through these moments of ecstasy, that that love is requited. John Calvin knew what he was rejecting when he preferred the peace of enlightenment over the passion of ecstasy, but later centuries have grown so tragically lost in the immediacy of bodily pleasure that viewers have come to lack the capacity even to imagine divine love.

---

[82] Walther Weiber, "The Representation of Ecstasy," in *Bernini in Perspective*, ed. George C. Bauer (Englewood Cliffs, NJ: Prentice-Hall, 1976), 81.

[83] Dan Brown, *Angels and Demons* (New York: Pocket Books, 2006), 336.

Chapter 13

SAINTS AND THEIR SPECIAL RELATIONSHIPS WITH CHRIST

Christianity burst upon the pagan world with an astounding message — God wanted a personal relationship with every man and woman in creation. Friendship with Christ conferred dignity on all humanity — slaves, women, the sick, and the disabled — a fact that was reflected in the art Christians had produced in the catacombs and in early churches. Protestant Reformers claimed that the personal nature of the relationship with the Lord had been usurped by intermediaries, particularly the clergy, but also the saints. Catholics, on the other hand, understood that holy men and women, whether martyrs or confessors, had enjoyed a special friendship with Christ, one that not only instructed, but also inspired, and that all disciples of Jesus belonged to one body, sharing in each other's gifts.

CONVERSION

The first and most essential step for this friendship to bloom was conversion. To turn away from the distractions of this world, to favor a relationship with Christ over any other, to conform one's

life to Jesus seemed overwhelming, especially in the age of post-
Reformation uncertainty. How to make that first fearful step of
following Christ attractive or, better yet, captivating?

Ask Caravaggio.

After a decade of painting still lifes in the shadows of Rome,
Caravaggio got his big break in 1599, when he was commissioned
to paint two canvasses of the life of St. Matthew for the French
church of St. Louis in Rome. The stakes were high. The king
of France, Henry IV, had just reverted to Catholicism the year
before, and the church was charged with preaching conversion
Masses to pilgrims during the year 1600. Furthermore, Caravaggio did not work in fresco, the preferred medium for mural painting, but would be working in the less prestigious oil on canvas.

Caravaggio played to his strengths in the commission, producing one of the most compelling scenes of conversion in the
history of art. In *The Calling of St. Matthew* the wealthy tax col-
lector sits at a table with his colleagues, counting the day's take.
Surprisingly, they do not wear the drapes and robes familiar to
biblical painting, but instead don contemporary dress. Caravaggio employed his still-life skills to render shimmering silk, lush
velvet, and luxurious brocade. A slim rapier rests in one man's
scabbard. These men appear to have all that one might desire:
money, status, comfort.

The scene is interrupted by two men dressed in simple woolen
robes, more consonant with the iconography of New Testament
scenes. They are barefoot, and the younger of the two, Jesus,
turns toward the table and points with a finger reminiscent of
Michelangelo's Adam in the Sistine Chapel's *Creation of Man*.

"Follow me," Jesus tells him (Matt. 9:9). The effect of these
words hits several of the men like a lightning bolt. One young
man jolts upward; the other youth seems to bask in the vision.

The Calling of St. Matthew by Caravaggio

Matthew however, recoils in shock. His finger turns toward himself as if to ask, "Who, me?" At first glance, Matthew does not appear eager to leave his belongings, his life, yet Caravaggio unveiled a new technique that reveals the rest of the story — light.

The powerful beam of light that projects from behind Jesus' head, the space of the altar in the chapel, hits St. Matthew full in the face. It is supernatural, since the window behind his head gives off no light. This light, the clarity of vision in which Matthew sees Jesus, the Way and the Truth, before him, is like an actor in the story, actively drawing the saint to his conversion and his vocation. Caravaggio later added the second figure, St. Peter, a little reminder of the importance of the Magisterium in connecting men to Christ.

Although it is never suggested by contemporaries, the modern age has begun to eschew the traditional identification of St. Matthew, preferring to see him in the boy with the bent head at the far end of the table. None of Caravaggio's peers or critics proposed such an idea, and it doesn't stand up to any kind of art historical methodology, yet this interpretation has gained momentum, seemingly even from Pope Francis himself.[84]

This alternate explanation neatly illustrates the difference between the modern age and that of the Catholic Restoration. The young man favored by twenty-first-century critics is absorbed in the here and now of counting the money before him. The light rests upon his head as if gently tapping him to look away from worldly pleasures. In this interpretation, Jesus would be standing before the supposed Matthew, patiently waiting for the boy to finish his business and decide to join Him. While this idea of the Lord waiting on sinners to complete their affairs before conversion is appealing, especially to an era like the present, the Catholic reform did not see conversion this way.

In the preceding chapter in Matthew, Jesus stressed the urgency of conversion when he told a young man who hesitated at His calling, "Follow me, and leave the dead to bury their own dead" (Matt. 8:22). Looking closely at Jesus' feet, the viewer can see that Christ is in motion; in a moment He will have already passed by, along with the personal invitation to conversion. Immediacy was the modus operandi of Caravaggio, as it was the mantra of the

---

[84] Cornelius Sullivan, "Pope Francis and Caravaggio," *Italian Insider,* September 25, 2013, http://www.italianinsider.it/?q=node/1694.

post-Reformation era. The pilgrims who walked the long way to see this work were already disposed in their hearts to find Christ should He walk by, just as Matthew had looked up from the table, searching for something more, just as Jesus walked by.

Caravaggio's work made conversion look like love at first sight, the first fear of change immediately replaced with the compelling light of truth.

CONTEMPLATION

In art, depicting the interaction between Christ and his saints had long been standard iconography. Sacred conversations, an arrangement of saints around Christ or the Madonna and Child were the norm in altarpieces and private devotional images. The compositions tended to be fairly staid, however. An array of devout figures stood prayerfully on the ground, with the sacred figure of Christ usually separated from them by a throne or, in older works, by an almond-shaped bubble rimmed with cherubs. A lucky donor or two might appear kneeling quietly in the corner, but the images mostly conveyed the idea of a carefully posed portrait of favorite saints.

In the Renaissance, Raphael started to explore a greater intermingling of the figures, floating down or rising up, but the Catholic Restoration took the old device of the sacred conversation and made it new. Santi di Tito, a Florentine painter, shook up the saintly ranks into a heady cocktail of holiness. His *Vision of St. Thomas Aquinas*, painted in 1573, was one of the first to be completed post Trent. Santi di Tito, considered "one of the most sensitive interpreters of Counter-Reformation art," not only anticipated Gabriele Paleotti's *Discourse on Sacred and Profane Images* by ten years in his didactic clarity, but he also produced this work "for his own devotion," or to enhance his personal relationship with Christ.[85] The Florence of Duke Cosimo I de' Medici had started slowly into the Counter-Reformation movement, even harboring in the earlier years several of the more noxious heretical teachers, but with the arrival of Pope Pius IV (a distant relative) and Pope Pius V (who conferred upon him the title of Grand Duke), he grew committed to restoring the Catholic Faith and was swift to implement the decrees of the council.

Santi di Tito certainly thought of his chosen profession more as a calling than as a job. He had joined the Confraternity of Thomas Aquinas in 1568 and enjoyed the respect of his peers and fellow citizens. Like Barocci, his use of color was poetic, with glistening pastel highlights and shadowy undertones, and like his fellow painters of the era, he believed that art should be charming but unambiguous.

Santi chose a moment from the life of Thomas Aquinas. The saint was in Naples, praying before the crucifix, when Christ on the Cross spoke to him, saying, "You have written well of me, Thomas. What would you want me to give you?" Thomas answered, "Nothing but You, Lord." His lifetime of dedication to the study of Christ and the mysteries of salvation was rewarded with words of divine approval, an extraordinary privilege desired by all the faithful.

Santi placed the altar squarely before the viewer, a large crucifix surmounting the stone slab. The Cross occupies the overwhelming majority of the space, presenting a body of

---

[85] Ludovica Sebregondi, "Churches, Convents, Monasteries and Confraternities in Counter Reformation Florence," in *The Cinquecento in Florence: "Modern Manner" and Counter-Reformation*, ed. Carlo Falciani and Antonio Natali (Firenze: Mandragora, 2017), 114.

The Vision of St. Thomas Aquinas by Santi di Tito

Christ that does not appear carved of wood or cast in bronze but made of flesh—weighty and real. St. Thomas's relationship with Christ, seen particularly in his teachings on transubstantiation and the poetic hymns the Angelic Doctor wrote to the Body and Blood of Christ, is rendered visible and real. The viewer is invited close to Christ as well—indeed, there seems to be a space waiting. Jesus turns slightly toward his dear friend Thomas. Further back in the church, Thomas's confreres gesture excitedly. They are watching, reveling even in the sight, but also learning from this special relationship between Christ and their brother.

COMPREHENSION

Catholic Restoration artists also found the subject of the Resurrection well suited to exploring the nature of friendship with Christ. This was the fruit of a slow development, since, in the earliest centuries, Jesus' return from the dead posed challenges to Christian art. Paleo-Christian artists avoided the subject altogether, perhaps out of respect for the Gospels' scant detail in describing the actual event.

Eventually Christ's return from death grew into a popular depiction, and artistic imagination began to supply what the scriptural account lacked. From dazzling mosaics to solemn frescoes, the kingly Christ stepping out of His tomb amid sleeping soldiers seemed to reconcile the different Gospel accounts. No human had seen Jesus' exit from the tomb, but thanks to art, the privileged viewer did.

The Renaissance era, with its love of action and emotion, took liberties with the subject. Rearing horses and fleeing soldiers seemed to undermine the quiet mystery of the empty tomb found on Easter morning by a few mourning women.

The Middle Ages had codified the interpretation of Scripture into four types — literal, moral, allegorical, and anagogical. Primacy had been given to the literal, notably by St. Thomas Aquinas, but the triumphalism of the Renaissance produced artistic renderings that even the wildest reading of Matthew's Gospel would not have produced. Matteo da Lecce's rough-and-ready version and Bronzino's supremely affected work drifted from the solemnity of the triumph over death to something that looked more like a Renaissance rave.

Even as the Protestant Reformers promoted strictest literal adherence to the Gospel, the climate of *sola scriptura* saw paradoxically a proliferation of biblical interpretations, leading the faithful further from the traditional understanding of Scripture, sacraments, saints, and salvation. As Swiss Reformer Samuel Werenfels put it:

As Men open this book, their favorite creed in mind;
Each seeks his own, and each his own doth find.[86]

In the face of increasingly audacious Catholic variants on Christ's Resurrection, the Church feared that artists were taking the same kind of interpretive liberties with Scripture as the Protestants were. Ultimately, the question arose whether Catholics should sponsor art that seemed to be more a part of the problem than the solution.

But in Christ, all things are made new, and therefore, the Catholic Church affirmed her support of the visual arts, demanding, however, clarity and accuracy in the artists' work. Cardinal

---

[86] Catholic University of America, *New Catholic Encyclopedia*, 2nd ed., 15 vols. (Detroit: Thomson/Gale, 2003), s.v. "Biblical Exegesis."

Federico Borromeo, like his cousin the great St. Charles, also penned a treatise; he wrote on painting and specifically lamented "the grave error of painting the resurrection of the Savior."[87]

"Indeed," he continued, "they represent Christ rising from the tomb in a way where the soldiers fall to the ground and pose shocked and frozen by the sudden event. This is false and erroneous."[88]

To portray Christ's Resurrection without intense human reactions seemed impossible for artists, but the era of the Catholic Restoration provided an environment that would spur their creativity. Painters started to focus on other events on the day of the Resurrection, especially Jesus' encounter with His friend Mary Magdalene outside the sepulcher. This scene allowed artists to explore the marvel of experiencing Jesus returned from the dead in a new, provocative way. The amazement portrayed was not that of those who had never believed, but of His followers and dearest friends, with whom many of the viewers could identify.

Painters from Albani to Zuccari had wrestled with the story of Christ's meeting with the Magdalene (John 20:11–17), but one of the most poignant Catholic Restoration images of *Noli Me Tangere* was painted by Lavinia Fontana in 1581. The first professional female painter in Catholic history, Lavinia found her greatest supporters among churchmen, particularly Archbishop Gabriele Paleotti of Bologna. For Lavinia, a commission to produce this image of the woman who was "the Apostle to the Apostles" must have held special significance.

---

[87] Federico Borromeo, *Sacred Painting: Museum*, ed. and trans. Kenneth Sprague Rothwell, Tatti Renaissance Library (Cambridge, MA: Harvard University Press, 2010), 15.

[88] Ibid.

Noli Me Tangere by Lavinia Fontana

Fontana's version emphasized accuracy: Mary Magdalene mistakes Jesus for a gardener; thus, the artist depicted Christ in a broad-brimmed hat, holding a shovel. Having emphasized the literal sense, Lavinia was free to evoke a beautiful scene. The atmosphere is permeated with warm golden light symbolic of the new age dawning. A little flashback scene in the distance shows the women arriving at the tomb, where an angel tells them Christ is gone. Mary's pose in the farther scene shows her with the slumped shoulders of dejection, but in the foreground her face becomes radiant with hope. Christ puts out His hand, ostensibly to tell her not to touch Him, but also in a gesture of affectionate blessing. Mary's gaze is directed toward the wound on His hand, made visible for her, but she seems to look beyond it, trying to gaze at His face under the shadowy brim. Proof of His Resurrection is not her primary concern as she sinks to her usual place by His feet in an attempt to embrace Him. The intimate nature of this scene, where the devoted friend basks in the joy of Christ's return and His reciprocation of her friendship, offers the faithful a view of what a personal relationship with Christ is like. The light, setting, and positions evoke a love story, a persuasive visual language that will continue well into the Baroque era.

At the very moment the Protestant Reformers were promising a more immediate, personal experience of Christ through Scripture, the Catholic Church was drawing on that very Scripture to produce artwork that emphasized the intimate, transformative encounter of the faithful with the Lord.

Chapter 14

PURGATORY

"A Roman swindle," "a papal fairy tale," "a deadly fiction of Satan," and "an offense against Christ and His Cross" were but a few of the epithets hurled at the ancient doctrine of Purgatory during the Protestant Reformation. Every famous Reformer took aim at the teaching, beginning with Luther, who, on the milder end of the scale, was concerned that it was unsubstantiated by Scripture. By the time the Thirty-Nine Articles of the Church of England were published, they condemned "the Romish Doctrine concerning purgatory" as "a fond thing, vainly invented, and grounded upon no warranty of Scripture, but rather repugnant to the Word of God."[89] Heterodox theologians reveled in dismantling the age-old relationship between the souls in this world and those in the next, from Bernardino Ochino to Peter Martyr Vermigli, whose namesakes, Franciscan and Dominican preachers against heresy, would have been scandalized to see their names associated with teaching that abandoned the faithful to the limitations of this world and broke the bonds with the loved ones who had preceded them in death.

[89] Baker, *A Plain Exposition*, 122.

The ties between the living and the souls in Purgatory had been cemented over the years. While Scripture scholars argued over references in 2 Maccabees 12 or Tobias 4:18 or Matthew 5:26 ("Truly, I say to you, you will never get out till you have paid the last penny"), everyday people had maintained ties with deceased loved ones through prayers, Masses, and practices intended to assist the "suffering souls." Art owes some of its greatest masterpieces to chapels dedicated to the souls of sinners, and as the days shortened in November, the faithful staved off the dread of the ensuing cold and dark by dedicating the month to remembering the dead.

The Church pressed her home-court advantage regarding Purgatory, first with theologians and then with art. St. Robert Bellarmine, who had taken it upon himself to respond point by point to every Protestant heresy, dedicated a book to Purgatory, with all teachings false and true, past and present, contained within its pages.

The Council of Trent asserted that there is a Purgatory, and that "the souls there detained are helped by the suffrages of the faithful, but principally by the acceptable sacrifice of the altars."[90] This decree was made in the final session of Trent on December 4, 1563, the same meeting that called for the continued support of the arts. As once Dante in *The Divine Comedy* had ingrained in the minds of readers the images of souls bent with pride or sprinting to purge sloth in his poetic *Purgatorio*, painters and sculptors were to help the faithful visualize Purgatory. Artists welcomed this challenge of rendering the invisible vivid and real, producing numerous remarkable works.

[90] Trent, *Canons and Decrees*, 299.

STAIRWAY TO HEAVEN

In preparation for the Jubilee Year 1600, when an astonishing 1.5 million pilgrims made their way to the Eternal City, Pope Clement VIII commissioned Caravaggio, Barocci, the Carracci, and every other gifted artist to create works that would both delight and teach the pilgrims. His nephew, Cardinal Pietro Aldobrandini, took it upon himself to make another contribution, in architecture, at the site of St. Paul's martyrdom, the Abbey of the Three Fountains. The cardinal not only rebuilt the church resting on the place where the Apostle to the Gentiles had been decapitated, his severed head bouncing three times and leaving each time a miraculous spring of water in its wake, but he also completed another church on the site, Santa Maria della Scala Coeli — Our Lady, Ladder to Heaven.

Begun in 1582 under Cardinal Alessandro Farnese, who had just finished financing the Gesù for the Jesuits, the church commemorated a Mass celebrated on the site by St. Bernard of Clairvaux in 1138 specifically for the souls of the dead. During the Mass, in the presence of Pope Innocent II, the saint saw a vision of souls released from Purgatory and ascending a ladder into Heaven with the assistance of angels. This vision undoubtedly played a part in forming Dante's poetic imagination when he described Purgatory in *The Divine Comedy* as seven stairwells hewn into rock.

In his writings on the *Canticle of Canticles* and his ecstatic meditations on divine love, St. Bernard dedicated a sermon to the "new Heretics" who "do not believe there remains after death the fire of purgatory, but allege that when the soul is released from the body it passes straight to rest or to damnation."[91] John

---

[91] *St. Bernard's Sermons on the Canticle of Canticles* (Dublin: Browne and Nolan, 1920), 272.

Calvin knew and cited St. Bernard in his work; therefore, the great Cistercian reformer seemed the worthiest figure to correct the errors of the Protestant Reformer who denounced Purgatory as "a deadly device of Satan."[92]

Cardinal Aldobrandini completed the church using an octagonal plan, the shape of the ancient baptisteries, like that at St. John Lateran. The eight sides were meant to represent the seven days of creation and the eighth for redemption. The entry was approached by a high stairway, recalling Bernard's vision. Inside were three altars: one honoring Mary in the Annunciation, the second commemorating St. Zeno and companions (martyrs whose relics were enshrined in the crypt), and the third was the sanctuary dedicated to the vision. The apse was decorated in a rare use of mosaic—obsolete and expensive by this time—but Francesco Zucchi was able to execute the *Madonna and Child with Sts. Bernard and Robert Molesme* (founder of the Cistercians) to the left and Sts. Vincent and Anastasius (titulars of the Lombard church across the way) on the right. The extended genesis of the work can be seen by the motif of the Farnese lilies around the border, but the portraits of Pope Clement VIII and Cardinal Aldobrandini, which flanked this sacred conversation, indicate that the work was completed for the pilgrims of 1600.

Purgatorius Ignis

Ludovico Carracci, the cofounder of the Carracci school, painted his Purgatory in 1610. He used a strikingly vivid and frontal composition for the altarpiece, emphasizing a more didactic element in the work. Both Bernardino Ochino and Peter Martyr Vermigli

---

[92] Calvin and Beveridge, *Institutes of the Christian Religion*, 576.

Santa Maria Scala Coeli, façade

had spent time in Bologna, and Vermigli had even been vicar of a local parish; therefore, Ludovico's painting was most likely meant to rebut any damage done by the heretical duo.

An Angel Frees the Souls of Purgatory by Ludovico Carracci

In the lower part of the painting, Ludovico used his loose brushstrokes and his mastery of color to depict flames breaking forth from a rocky bed. The *purgatorius ignis*, necessary for cleansing the soul, had been described by Pope Gregory the Great in the sixth century and remained the most powerful image of purification of the afterlife. Men and women, equally consumed by the flames, beg for release. These figures appear to emerge from the space of the altar where Masses were to be said for their souls. An angel clad in the gold and white that would come to symbolize the state of grace in the Baroque era rises from the flames, grasping one of the sufferers by the hand. Pointing upward, the angel explicitly points to St. Augustine, who wrote the *Treatise on Caring for the Dead*. Sitting with the Doctor of the Church are several other saints associated with teachings on Purgatory, from Sts. Francis and Dominic to St. Nicholas of Tolentino and the soon-to-be-canonized Philip Neri, well known for his concern for the souls of the dead. The last figure hidden toward the back seems to be a scriptural figure, perhaps St. Matthew or one of the Maccabees, the two biblical texts most invoked for proof of Purgatory. Even as Masses were offered for the dead, Ludovico's altarpiece affirmed the continuity of the teaching on Purgatory from the earliest Church to the contemporary age.

ALTARE PRIVILEGIATUM

Back in the sixth century, the indefatigable Gregory the Great gave the Church her clearest teaching on Purgatory. So celebrated for his preoccupation with souls that legend had it that he had successfully prayed to release the soul of the pagan emperor Trajan from Hell, Gregory dedicated much attention to describing Purgatory and how to assist souls suffering therein. One case, described in his *Dialogues*, involved a monk named Justus, who had died with the burden of the sin of avarice still staining his soul. Gregory, moved by compassion, hoped to assist him in the afterlife, and together with his brother priests he dedicated thirty consecutive Masses in suffrage for Justus's soul. After the last liturgy, Justus appeared to his brother Copiousus (who was unaware of Gregory's intercessory Masses) and recounted how he had been freed from Purgatory.[93] Thus, the custom of the thirty Gregorian Masses took root. Special altars were designated for these requiem Masses and even today, the inscription *Altare Privilegiatum* can be seen in churches throughout Europe, indicating that a plenary indulgence could be gained for a soul in Purgatory when Mass was celebrated there.

In 1617, Giovanni Battista Crespi was commissioned to paint the story of Pope Gregory and Justus for the Church of St. Victor in Varese, near Milan. The church was rebuilt as a headquarters of Catholic teaching in the Post-Reformation era, following the prescriptions of Charles Borromeo. With a chapel dedicated to the Rosary and an altar frontal commemorating the Battle of Lepanto, the church proudly proclaimed its orthodoxy. Crespi, friend to Cardinal Federico Borromeo, painted the altarpiece for the *Altare Privilegiatum* of the church. Crespi had been in Rome at the cusp of the Holy Year of 1600 and was attracted by the nascent tenebrist style. His image of St. Gregory the Great freeing the soul of Justus bears the marks of his study of both Caravaggio and the Carracci. The zigzag composition erupts from the lower left in a burst of Ludovico-like flames. The eye rises through a

---

[93] *The Dialogues of Saint Gregory, Surnamed the Great; Pope of Rome and the First of That Name. Divided into Four Books, Wherein He Entreateth of the Lives and Miracles of the Saints in Italy and of the Eternity of Men's Souls*, ed. Edmund G. Gardner (London: P. L. Warner, 1906), 250–252.

St. Gregory Delivers the Soul of a Monk by Giovanni Battista Crespi

tangle of sorrowful figures, some shouting, some succumbing to their punishments, but all gazing upward. Crespi used russet tones to depict these men and women, the colors of the flesh. The next series of figures are painted with more luminosity, as if they have been purified of the worldliness and are ready to rise. Angels, ever present amid things divine, assist these people to Heaven.

Off to the left, a little window opens upon a tidy church interior with Pope Gregory celebrating Mass with a little group of priests. The Host and chalice are clearly visible and appear to float before the raised hands of the celebrant. A wispy white ribbon seems to rise from the sacrament to the open heavens to become a flowing banner inscribed with the words of the Requiem: *Fac eas, Domine, de morte transire ad vitam* (Grant them, O Lord, to pass from death to life). Crespi added more angels, painted with a delicate stroke that anticipates Impressionism by 250 years, circling the golden area of Heaven. Crespi's work invited the faithful to think about both tradition and mystery, inciting viewers to imagine that they, too, were sharing in the visions of the great saints from Gregory to Bernard to St. Rose of Lima.

Part III

COOPERATION

<hr>

All the world's a stage,
And all the men and women merely players;
They have their exits and their entrances,
And one man in his time plays many parts.

—William Shakespeare, *As You Like It*, Act II, Scene VII

No one is immune to the theatrical appeal of the Eternal City. The surprise of an airy piazza nestled within a web of alleys, the lively spurt of water amid figures, animals, or exotic obelisks, and the buildings, peopled with statues, invite visitors to play a part in the existential drama unfolding around them.

The dazzled tourist, agog at the wonders of Rome, rarely perceives that the transformation of the city into a glorious proscenium took place during the Catholic Restoration. The Church set out to engage every pilgrim, tourist, diplomat, or dissident who crossed her portals and sweep him up in a great rhetorical display that wove together the many threads of the urban fabric. The Catholic Restoration made its most winning appeal to the heart and mind in the arts and layout of Rome. William Shakespeare's works were at the time mere seedlings on the European literary landscape, but the taste for drama had taken root in Rome and flourished in the sets and stages constructed throughout the city.

In reorganizing roads, piazzas, and fountains, the papacy was particularly motivated by the increasing influx of pilgrims arriving in Rome. The celebration of "Holy Years" had floundered during the Reformation, but by the end of the sixteenth century, the faithful were returning to see the sacred sites of Rome. Among the ranks of the pilgrims were some who had been exposed for their entire lives to Protestant teachings and carried with them much doubt and confusion about truth in Christian teaching. These perplexities were addressed in art as well as preaching in the Eternal City.

The theme of Restoration Rome was one of welcome. Where many Protestant states brooked no opposition, mandating that the faithful attend state-sponsored services and prohibiting any texts that might contradict the teachings of the prevailing national Protestant theology, the Catholic Church understood doubt and attempted to make the visitor feel that he was not alone in the struggle to find the correct course.[94]

To that end, the city was redesigned with roads leading to the most venerable churches, and accessorized with sparkling fountains at the major crossroads, inviting the traveler to refresh the body along with the mind. Piazzas opened off the stretches of long, straight streets, laid out to guide pilgrims to their sacred destination. Like delightful oases, the musical splash of a

---

[94] The Catholic Church also had an *Index of Prohibited Books*; the index being produced in Rome, however, meant that many of the prelates had read the books and were able to explain the problems and the heresies within.

fountain, the monumental posturing of a statue, and the curvilinear façade of a church all evoked the joy that accompanies faith.

The city's layout privileged pilgrimage, the great Catholic activity so forcefully discouraged by Protestants. Those who embarked on this journey of love were rewarded by finding a city organized for them. The Church knew that it wasn't just the faithful who were swelling her streets, however, as more and more non-Catholics arrived in Rome. The expansion and exploration of the globe from the time of Martin Luther to the Jubilee of 1600 had been overwhelming. The Church was in the midst of forging diplomatic contacts with distant countries, from Japan to Peru, with the aim of bringing the Gospel to every corner of the world. The decoration of piazzas and churches reflected that outreach, whether in presenting exotic geographic locales in the fountains and frescoes or the inclusion of different ethnic types—African, Asian, Semitic, South American—in the altarpieces. Globalization became a reality in the seventeenth century, and the Church chose to invest heavily in one of its most effective vehicles for evangelization: beauty.

Discoveries on earth went hand in hand with speculation regarding the heavens. The development of the telescope, and the increasing dependence on empirical knowledge saw university professors become rock stars in this era. The Church and the faithful struggled to navigate the delicate balance between what can be known through the senses and what must be discerned with the heart. Art had an important role to play in illustrating the subtleties of these questions and produced surprising ways to engage scholars and citizens alike in this great intellectual conversation.

On a more tangible level, however, the city was rife with evidence of the long history of the Roman Church and the centuries of witness soaked into her soil. The serendipitous rediscovery of the Catacombs of Priscilla, with its thousands of men, women, children, popes, and martyrs laid to rest within, began the process of recovering the dozens of sites where the earliest Christian community awaited the Last Judgment. Relics and inscriptions joined forces with paintings and sculptures to profess the ancient truths of the Catholic Faith.

In an era of persecution and strife, the people resting in the catacomb graves had made a choice to believe in Christ. In many cases the decision had cost them their lives, and those tombs were marked with hastily painted figures in prayerful thanks or a palm frond to denote one of "Heaven's athletes" who had crossed the finish line. The pilgrims of the Catholic Restoration had something in common with this ancient community: they, too, had made a choice.

The Protestant Reformation had introduced the faithful to the seductive illusion of options. First Luther, then Calvin, Zwingli, Melanchthon, Henry VIII, and many others presented more "choices" of how to interpret and live out revelation in one's life. The state-established churches, such as Calvin's Geneva and Elizabeth's England, however, left their citizens no alternatives; so, like the early martyrs who opted to cling to Christ in the face of imperial persecution, men and women such as St. Thomas More and the remarkable St. Margaret Clitherow chose Catholicism and accepted the consequences.

The populations of the post-Reformation era faced an overwhelming amount of information. The sermons, pamphlets, and relentless campaigns of the vying faiths apprised the faithful of the many interpretations of Scripture, so the laypeople were given what was, at least, the semblance of an informed choice. Everyone agreed that God's grace was freely given, and all humanity was redeemed through Christ's sacrifice, but people had to decide how they would work with that gift. The Council of Trent called the faithful "to convert themselves to their own justification," by "freely assenting to and co-operating with" grace.[95] The Protestants had varying interpretations on how to live justification "by faith alone." These individual choices, however, meant that every person would be responsible for his decision, whether it led to martyrdom or to worldly glory, and of course, for the subsequent effects of that choice in the afterlife.

This was a heady responsibility for the faithful—a share in the control of the destiny of their own souls. This aspect of the Reformation became an artistic playground—where creativity and formal innovation met in the most beautiful of ways. From the dawn of the Renaissance, making art was about choice— to add here, to reduce there, which color and what size; the finished work was always a result of careful selections, and the artist's ability to exercise "good judgment."[96] Michelangelo, Raphael, and Leonardo had become giants thanks to their often surprisingly innovative decisions regarding what to paint or not to paint.

A new generation of innovators would appear on the art scene—able to illustrate the difficulty of selecting the right path while stressing the importance of this decision. One of these innovators was the turbulent Caravaggio, in and out of prison, constantly struggling against the darkness of sin and reflecting his spiritual battles in his art. The modern age has tried to kidnap this "bad boy" painter as a worldly maverick too cynical to worry about salvation, but what makes his art so powerful even today is precisely his battle to find light in ever-encroaching darkness.

---

[95] Trent, *Canons and Decrees*, 59.
[96] Vasari, *The Lives of the Artists*, 250.

Women also shot to the forefront of art—respectable married women such as Lavinia Fontana, who produced altarpieces throughout Europe, as well as women who had fallen under shadow due to scandal, such as Artemisia Gentileschi. They, too, were encouraged to use their talents and their experience to engage and convert the faithful. All in all, this was a thrilling time for art and artists as they vied to take the ancient teachings and render them new, yet unaltered, for this dynamic age.

Images proliferated. The immense variety was designed to appeal to a broad range of viewers, and yet, in the words of the Elizabethan bard, "there's the rub." The beauty, the encyclopedic array of scenes and styles, were intended not only to delight the viewers but also to engage them. The empty space in a Caravaggio painting drew the beholder into the scene, while the raised proscenium of a church's façade also served as a reminder that every person is called to bear witness to Christ in his life. Art no longer allowed the viewer to stand at a safe distance, as a passive recipient of grace, but exhorted everyone to act, to perform, or, in answer to Hamlet's famous dilemma, "to be."

"To be" meant vigilance against the ever-present temptations of sin, which, at times, arrived in seductive guise and, on other occasions, attacked in an onslaught of vehemence and ugliness that appeared impossible to overcome. Art depicted the brutality of the war on sin in gritty violent images, illustrating saintly men and women who had defeated evil before them. The Tridentine fathers had warned that holiness would not be easy, and art rose to evoke this challenge.

"Let those who think themselves to stand, take heed lest they fall, and, with fear and trembling work out their salvation, in labors, in watchfulness, in almsgiving, in prayers and oblations, in fasting and chastity," Trent counseled, "for, knowing that they are born again unto a hope of glory, but not as yet unto glory, they ought to fear for the combat which yet remains with the flesh, with the world, with the devil, wherein they cannot be victorious, unless they be with God's grace."[97]

The faithful were to take heart and gather courage through the sacraments, preaching, and yes, even pictures that provided visual models and inspiration.

Art inspired the Catholic faithful to be protagonists in their own salvation, to cooperate with the unearned grace that they were given by performing acts of mercy and living out the gospel freely and joyfully. Every moment mattered, every word counted, every action was accountable, and by making choices to increase piety and reduce vice, to polish with prayer or color with charity, Catholics became works of art in and of themselves.

The ultimate goal of the theater of life was not the approval of peers or the awards that might be conferred by the contemporary culture. Each Catholic actor had only one goal — to make his performance resemble the life of Jesus. Every artistic interpretation of a Christlike life would be different, and together they formed a magnificent gallery of holiness as seen in the lives of the saints.

Shakespeare's *Macbeth* laments that life is "a poor player, that struts and frets his hour upon the stage, and then is heard no more."[98] The angry, cynical words of a man who chose evil were transformed by the Catholic Restoration to lend significance to every moment of life, as a chance to choose the good, to act, to participate, and to perform with an eye to joining the great cast of Heaven.

---

[97] Trent, *Canons and Decrees*, 56.
[98] *Macbeth*, Act V, Scene 5.

Chapter 15

DOUBT

Like the sudden storms on the sea of Galilee, Rome was rocked by powerful gales of doubt in the wake of the Protestant Reformation. Martin Luther's initial rejection of relics, pious traditions, and penitential practice had taken place on Rome's Holy Stairs when he decided that "the just shall live by faith alone." Soon after, Reformers would deny the Real Presence in the Eucharist, along with the role of the papacy and the Magisterium as well as the necessity of human cooperation in personal salvation. Doubt engulfed the faithful, and the barque of Peter seemed to be fracturing into an ever-increasing number of pieces. Christians wondered which plank to cling to for eternal life. With doubt came darkness and loneliness, which threatened to cast a pall over the Eternal City.

There are few areas where the Catholic Church responded as beautifully and compassionately through art as she did to the problem of doubt. Both public and private works emphasized the universality of human uncertainty, all the while underscoring the importance of maintaining the faith even during the most unsettling squalls.

St. Peter and Doubt

St. Peter's Basilica became the first space actively to address the problem of doubt through art. Built on the tomb of the first pope, who had experienced fear, denial, and disbelief, yet had doggedly returned to offer his life in witness to the truth of Christ, the new basilica had just been completed with Michelangelo's magnificent dome in 1590. The decorative plan was entrusted to the Oratorian cardinal Cesare Baronio, author of a new Church history and editor of the Roman martyrology.

Cardinal Baronius decided to confront the issue of doubt at the very threshold of the church. The old basilica had boasted the "Navicella" mosaic designed by Giotto in the entrance courtyard. Seen by countless pilgrims, it illustrated the Gospel scene in which Peter, seeing Christ walking upon the waters of the stormy sea of Galilee, asked Him:

> "Lord, if it is you, bid me come to you on the water." He said, "Come." So Peter got out of the boat and walked on the water and came to Jesus; but when he saw the wind, he was afraid, and beginning to sink he cried out, "Lord, save me." Jesus immediately reached out his hand and caught him, saying to him, "O man of little faith, why did you doubt?" (Matt. 14:28–31)

In Giotto's version from 1310, the crisis has passed: Peter holds the hand of Christ, who looks calmly toward the viewer as the storm subsides. Baronius kept the older image in the courtyard of the new basilica, but for the side entrance, reserved for clergy, he commissioned a new version by Bernardo Castello in 1604 (repainted by Lanfranco in 1627). This new work is more turbulent, with high waves and agitated apostles on the boat.

Altar of the Navicella by Giovanni Lanfranco, 1628;
original painting by Bernardo Castello, 1604

Peter is sinking, but Jesus clasps his wrist while pointing upward toward the first glimmer of serene skies.

This dynamic depiction greeted the clergy just as they entered the church, encouraging them to leave doubt outside these

Altar of St. Thomas the Apostle, by Vincenzo Camuccini,
1806; original painting by Domenico Passignano, 1622

doors. If the shepherds are not sure-footed, what will happen to
the sheep?

ST. THOMAS AND DOUBT

Baronius highlighted the theme of doubt again, commissioning
an image of Doubting Thomas for another altar in St. Peter's,

closer to the tomb. The present work was originally painted by Domenico Passignano in 1622 and shows a somewhat staid image of the standing Christ as Thomas reaches toward the wound in his side, while two other apostles huddle over his shoulder. The altar crucifix projects itself into the space between Thomas and Christ, a reminder of what caused those wounds. Jesus, for His part, faces Thomas, yet His body is turned frontally toward the viewer. His side is bared toward Thomas, but his hands and feet are shown to the faithful, involving them in this moment of doubt. Passignano also painted the body of Jesus as exceptionally luminous, as if to remind viewers that He is the Light and the Truth.

CARAVAGGIO AND THE TWIN

St. Thomas and the problem of personal doubt was better suited to intimate works than to large altarpieces, however. Smaller canvases in private settings allowed the faithful to wrestle with their uncertainties and prepare themselves in the shelter of home for the tsunami of challenges that raged outside the door. Rubens, Guercino, and Mattia Preti were among the parade of painters who produced these images, but Caravaggio's *Incredulity of St. Thomas*, painted in 1602 for the influential Giustiniani brothers, remains the most compelling.

Caravaggio dramatically reduced the size of the image, opening a window on a cluster of four heads that form the shape of a cross. The bodies of the three apostles are lost in the shadows, drawing attention to only their faces. Christ, however, stands almost entirely visible before them. In the foreground, Thomas leans close to the wound. His brow is lifted in an astonished expression as Jesus guides his finger into His side. This graphic, even disturbing image — the gash in Christ's flesh accentuated

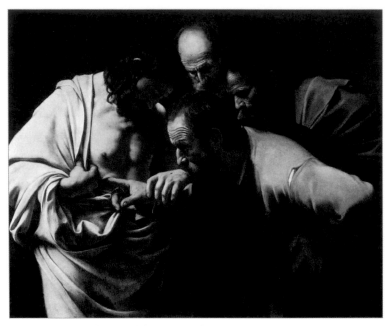

The Incredulity of St. Thomas by Caravaggio

by the rip in the shoulder of Thomas's tunic—vividly recalls the physical suffering that Jesus endured a week earlier. Yet here He stands serene, patient with his friend's doubt. From Jesus comes the light that will open Thomas's eyes.

Caravaggio's sympathy with Thomas is evident in the warm colors of gold, russet, and burnt orange—this is a true refuge where Jesus knows and accepts human limitations. The two apostles crowded over Thomas's shoulder suggest that he was not alone in his incredulity but was the only one who voiced it.

Perhaps Caravaggio's most powerful compositional device is the shadowy little space between Thomas and Christ. In Passignano's painting, it is occupied by the crucifix, but in this work, it is meant to be filled by the viewer. Thomas—the name means "twin"—invites each of us to take part in the scene and to hear Christ's words: "Have you believed because you have seen me? Blessed are those who have not seen and yet believe" (John 20:29).

DOUBT AND DESCARTES

Doubt grew more settled into the human condition when René Descartes developed an entire philosophical method around systematic doubt in the mid-seventeenth century. Undaunted, the Church responded with spectacular works of art. The culmination of the Roman Baroque saw the most perfect integration of Doubting Thomas into the very fabric of a church when St. John Lateran commissioned a series of fourteen-foot-tall statues of the apostles for its nave. The cathedral of Rome, the oldest legally built Christian church in the world, and a destination for every pilgrim in the Holy Years, had seen everything from natural disasters to internal implosions and knew how to contextualize doubt for the millions who crossed its threshold.

The statues were placed from 1680 to 1720 in the large piers lining the 450-foot nave that leads to the altar. In Christian church design, the nave, derived from the Latin word *navis*, meaning "boat," symbolizes the journey of the faithful in this ark of salvation. The apostles in their niches punctuate that journey, with Bartholomew holding his skin (a symbol of his having been flayed alive) and Matthew rejecting his bag of coins, each demonstrating his example of witness. Only one figure, however, protrudes aggressively from his niche to command the attention of the visitor—St. Thomas.

Pierre Le Gros started work on the colossal St. Thomas in 1705. Born in Paris, Le Gros had moved to Rome as a young sculptor and soon became one of the favorite artists of the Jesuit order. His sweeping drapery gave dramatic life and movement to the stone, following in the footsteps of Bernini, much missed after his death in 1680. Le Gros also arranged his figures in dynamic poses. Thomas is bent at the waist, and his foot juts out from the pedestal, while his head turns sharply as his lips part and his arm thrusts upward. The other hand holds an architect's square, an allusion to an apocryphal story that Thomas was invited to India as an architect and a carpenter.

Walking along the nave, the faithful simulated the journey of faith, beautifully described by Dante in *The Divine Comedy*. His epic poem opens with the line "In the middle of the journey of our life I found myself within a dark wood where the straight way was lost."[99] Like Dante, the faithful, assailed by doubt, were in danger of wandering off the straight way, until, halfway along the length of the basilica, they were met by St. Thomas, everyone's twin, thrusting out that famous finger to show them the way. For all his doubts and need for verification, St. Thomas was also the first apostle to proclaim, "My Lord and my God!" (John 20:28).

Instead of permitting doubt to create isolation among the faithful, the Church engaged with this very human phenomenon, common to believers and nonbelievers alike. The Catholic Restoration anticipated artistically what Cardinal Ratzinger would explain in words four hundred years later.

Both the believer and the unbeliever share, each in his own way, doubt and belief. Neither can quite escape either doubt or belief; for the one, faith is present against doubt, for the other through doubt and in the form of doubt. It

---

[99] Dante Alighieri, *The Divine Comedy*, trans. Allen Mandelbaum (Berkeley: University of California Press, 1980), vol. 1, canto 1, line 1.

is the basic pattern of man's destiny only to be allowed to find the finality of his existence in this unceasing rivalry between doubt and belief, temptation, and certainty. Perhaps in precisely this way doubt, which saves both sides from being shut up in their own worlds, could become the avenue of communication."[100]

The art of the post-Reformation Church, as the privileged form of communication, excels even today at drawing the believer and the nonbeliever side by side to share the experience of doubt as depicted by Caravaggio or sculpted by Le Gros.

---

[100] Pope Benedict XVI, *Introduction to Christianity* (San Francisco: Ignatius Press, 1990), 47.

Chapter 16

PILGRIMAGE: A
JOURNEY OF LOVE

Is there anything more compelling than a journey made for love? A surprise visit home for the holidays, a suitor arriving unexpectedly on bended knee, or Odysseus struggling nine long years to return to Penelope—travel undertaken for others has historically captured the imagination while warming the heart.

Pilgrimage is the ultimate journey of love: the steep cost in time, expense, and inevitable discomfort means that only a determined heart would undertake such an adventure. Many religions promoted pilgrimage throughout the centuries, but Christians gave it a special stamp of their own. From the moment Jesus exhorted His apostles, "Go therefore and make disciples of all nations, baptizing them in the name of the Father and of the Son and of the Holy Spirit, teaching them to observe all that I have commanded you" (Matt. 28:19–20), Christians have traveled the world not only to spread the gospel, but also to visit the sites where the story of salvation unfolded and where great saints bore witness to truth.

The hardship of pilgrimage—long treks on foot; unusual food or, worse yet, deprivation; danger of disease; and the threat of brigands—made the activity a form of penance, a true gesture of atonement. Given that pilgrims ran the risk of death, these journeys could be assigned as satisfaction for the most serious of sins.

The Reformation, however, called the practice of pilgrimage into question. Martin Luther scoffed that pilgrims were rarely motivated for the "right" reasons:

> Those who make pilgrimages do so for many reasons, very seldom for legitimate ones. The first reason for making pilgrimages is the most common of all, namely, the curiosity to see and hear strange and unknown things. This levity proceeds from a loathing for and boredom with the worship services, which have been neglected in the pilgrims' own church.[101]

Luther grew more disdainful of pilgrimage as the years went by, deriding the error of "those who run hither and yon for the purpose of becoming righteous," claiming that "they perform many outward works which glitter very nicely, but inwardly they remain full of malice."[102] Ultimately, at the end of his life, Luther condemned pilgrimage in no uncertain terms as sex tourism.[103]

The final session of the Council of Trent championed the Catholic tradition of pilgrimage and set about preparing for a Holy Year to encourage travelers to Rome. After the turbulent and dangerous years of the Reformation, which saw severely diminished numbers of visitors, the streets once again began to swell with the flow of pilgrims. In 1550, St. Philip Neri opened a hospice for pilgrims, which would become the Church of Santissima

---

[101] *Luther's Works on CD-ROM*, vol. 31, 198.
[102] Ibid., vol. 44, 86.
[103] Ibid., vol. 54, 422.

Trinità dei Pellegrini, where he and his volunteers cared for no fewer than 140,000 pilgrims in 1575, the first Holy Year after the close of Trent. St. Philip also encouraged the denizens of the Eternal City to join in a local pilgrimage to seven ancient churches spread throughout the city, a tradition that lives on to this day.

THE ROADS TO SALVATION

Post-Tridentine Rome worked intensely to welcome the returning pilgrims, thinking not only of spiritual transports but also temporal practicalities. One of the most lasting, yet unappreciated consequences of the Church's affirmation of pilgrimage was the urban layout of Rome, with its startling landmarks and ubiquitous fountains. Pope Sixtus V reigned a short five years yet embodied the theatrical spirit of the age by making every second count. Elected in 1585, a gardener's son who had tended pigs on his family farm before joining the Franciscan Order, Sixtus vigorously tackled the numerous problems of the city. He routed out brigandage, which had made the streets unsafe for both pilgrims and residents alike, then turned to the issue of clean water, building the Acqua Felice (see chapter 6). Sixtus's greatest contribution, however, was his long straight roads, which formed a network from the northern gate of the city all the way to the cathedral of Rome, pressed against the southern stretch of the ancient Aurelian Walls.

Sixtus started by linking St. Mary Major (destined to be the site of his tomb) to the Piazza del Popolo, the principal entry point for pilgrims, with a road bearing his Christian name, Felice. He eventually extended the road to include Santa Croce in Gerusalemme, the church that contained the precious relics of Christ's Passion. Via Merulana tied St. John Lateran and St. Mary Major together, while today's Piazza di Spagna would lead to Via della Ripetta (the primary route for St. Peter's in the Vatican) thanks to Via Trinitatis (now Via Condotti). Where once all roads had led to Rome, in Sixtus's city all roads led to the Blessed Virgin Mary.

Sixtus planned for Rome "to function efficiently as the greatest place of pilgrimage in the Christian world," taking personal pleasure in joining the pilgrims as they traveled his roads along St. Phillip's seven-churches walk.[104]

The most striking innovation of Sixtus's urban design was the use of obelisks to punctuate the important sites around the city. The Egyptian monoliths, looted by the Roman emperors, had first symbolized divine illumination for the pharaohs and later military might for the imperial armies. Sixtus recovered these obelisks, many buried after centuries of neglect, and re-erected them to even greater purpose.

The first obelisk was not unearthed but moved. The obelisk by St. Peter's Basilica had stood for fifteen hundred years since its transport to Rome by the emperor Caligula. It stood on the spina of the horse-racing circus where St. Peter had died, executed by Nero after the great fire of Rome. The tall column of granite had been present for the death of the Prince of the Apostles, and in 1586, Pope Sixtus decided to place this "silent witness" in front of the magnificent new basilica that he was completing. The task of moving the eighty-four-foot-long block 820 feet took architect Domenico Fontana from April 30 to September 10, 1586. The tireless pope then decided to reconstruct the other broken obelisks around the city, one at the Piazza del Popolo, another at St. Mary Major, and a third at St. John Lateran. Placed at the ends of his long avenues, they were visible at great distances, allowing

---

[104] Magnuson, *Rome in the Age of Bernini*, vol. 1, 19.

pilgrims to find their way from church to church much like "pins" on a map today. This navigation system, which functions to this day, owes its origin to Pope Sixtus's love of organization and St. Philip's love of pilgrims.

One of Philip Neri's favorite paintings represented a very special pilgrimage. Federico Barocci's *Visitation*, painted in 1586 in the Chiesa Nuova, shows Mary hurrying to Elizabeth immediately after the angel Gabriel tells her she will become the Mother of God. Elizabeth, too, is pregnant with John the Baptist, and Mary races to share this moment of divine love with her cousin.

Barocci entices the viewer into the story with the figure of Joseph reaching down to lift an opaque sack filled with bread and a metal ewer of wine. He appears to lean toward the viewer to gather these gifts from the liturgical space of the altar. On the right, a servant girl in a fetching color combination of lemon yellow, dusky rose, and olive green climbs the stair, holding a gift of two birds. Her straw hat and the woven basket have a high-definition quality that makes the scene appear crisply realistic.

Mary, a glorious example of humility, climbs the stairs toward her cousin, who waits in an archway as Zechariah emerges from the semidarkness. Barocci's strength was always color, able to both delight and awaken the senses. Mary moves amid the brightest of shades as she brings the Light into the world, but the world of Elizabeth lies in murky shadows. The Blessed Mother touches Elizabeth's arm, and the first splash of brilliant tint spreads along the sleeve. Barocci employs color to illustrate the baby "leaping" in Elizabeth's womb and her being filled with the Holy Spirit. The joyous, almost intoxicating hues of the painting deeply affected St. Philip, who experienced one of his visions while praying before the work.

The Visitation by Federico Barocci

MOTHER OF PILGRIMS

The Jubilee Year 1600 was expected to be particularly successful with an estimated half million people coming to the Eternal
City. Pope Clement VIII, amid his many preparations, made a
personal pilgrimage to the Holy House of Loreto, believed to
be the transported site of the Annunciation. In one journey,
he both affirmed the value of pilgrimage and underscored the
church's abiding confidence in the intercession of the Blessed
Virgin Mary.

Four years later, Caravaggio was commissioned to paint the
Madonna of Loreto, also known as *Madonna of the Pilgrims*, for the
personal chapel of Ermete Cavaletti, a habitual volunteer at St.
Philip's pilgrim center. Executed for the Church of Sant'Agostino,
a major stopping point on the congested route of Via dei Coro-
nari, this startling painting bore none of the charming color in
Barocci's painting; instead it greeted visitors with two pilgrims in
threadbare clothes, thrusting dirty bare feet toward the viewer.
Soiled trousers, callouses, and a hefty gluteus maximus still take
tourists by surprise in this first image one sees when entering the
chapel on the left.

But as any footsore traveler can tell you, in Rome, legs are the
most reliable form of conveyance. In this picture, after hundreds
of miles, the man and woman can finally park their "cars," sinking down and resting at their destination. The walking sticks
separate the faces from the ungainly bodies, however, and their
expressions tell a very different story. Caravaggio reveals only
a tantalizing sliver of their faces, but the woman breaks into an
apple-cheeked grin, her wrinkles emanating like rays of light. In
the man's face, all lines disappear in the bright light, which em-
phasizes the wide-open eyes that seem to grow in astonishment.
Whatever they have come to see, they have found it.

Madonna of the Pilgrims by Caravaggio

It is clearly not the building, painted with peeling plaster revealing cheap brick and nicks in the stone doorway; they have journeyed out of love, and they have found love waiting for them. Caravaggio hints that the Madonna and Child before them is an apparition. The hefty child could not possibly be held by Mary resting lightly on the tips of her toes, and Mary's robe shimmers like silk and velvet; the pilgrims are experiencing a brief mystical moment amid the heaviness of everyday existence.

This joyful composition leaves an unsettling feeling, nonetheless. It appears to form a triangle—Mary at the apex, the pilgrims to the right, and a gaping space to the left by the entrance door. This space once again seems to be reserved for the viewers, who are perhaps coming to see the work for its fame rather than its content. These tourists—the curious or the superficial, who have "come to see and hear strange and unknown things"—see Jesus' face in shadow and are left with a longing to be brought into the privileged position of the humble pilgrims.[105] They may be unkempt and uncouth, yet in their simple faith, Mary favors them, leaning down to form a visual bridge to her Son.

The work sparked outrage among many visitors, and accusations of a lack of decorum were championed by Caravaggio's rival painters and detractors, along with the rumor that the model for the Virgin Mary had been a girlfriend of Caravaggio: Lena, "who stood in Piazza Navona," a euphemism for a prostitute.[106] But in truth it doesn't take much to see where the model came from, since the straight lines of the face and the thick, wavy hair parted in the center are the defining features of the statue of

---

[105] *Luther's Works on CD-ROM*, vol. 31, 198.
[106] Howard Hibbard, *Caravaggio*, Icon Editions (New York: Harper and Row, 1983), 191.

Our Lady of Safe Delivery carved by Jacopo Sansovino in 1520, placed just ten yards away.

It is hard to look one's best externally during a pilgrimage — indeed, lost luggage, food sickness, and the inability to communicate with locals are all part of the humiliations that one undergoes during these journeys — but Caravaggio sought to express that, while doing nothing for the outer appearance, pilgrimage helps one to shine more brightly within.

Chapter 17

GLOBALIZATION, CATHOLIC STYLE

---✳︎---

Globalization may seem a concept of the new millennium, fostered by social media and multinational businesses, but the Catholic Church realized the importance of uniting the different peoples of an ever-expanding world long before Facebook was even a twinkle in Mark Zuckerberg's eye.

Martin Luther tapped into the capillaries of Europe through his use of the printing press, disseminating pamphlets by the thousands, and by 1519 he was the most published author in Europe. He swiftly learned how to manipulate this medium, using his characteristic vitriolic language that would be considered "clickbait" today, as well as commissioning devastating satirical images of the pope as the Antichrist and composing rousing anti-Catholic ballads. As Luther jousted and jeered and journeyed through Europe, Rome had her eye farther afield. For every explorer's voyage, looking for new trade routes and rich resources, missionaries were not far behind, ready to offer their lives to bring the good news to these new peoples who had never heard the name of Jesus.

In 1511, Pope Julius II had established the first Roman Catholic diocese in the New World in Santo Domingo, with the intention of bringing the gospel to these far reaches of the planet, unknown to Europe until only a few years earlier. While the immediate crisis of the Protestant Reformation had slowed evangelical efforts, the papacy did not take long to rediscover its missionary zeal and focus on these new frontiers.

In 1537, Pope Paul III asserted himself as the defender of the human dignity of indigenous people when, in his encyclical *Sublimus Dei*, he decried the greed of some merchant explorers who "are presuming to assert far and wide that the Indians ... be reduced to slavery like brute animals, under the pretext that they are lacking the Catholic faith." Invoking his apostolic authority, Paul decreed and declared "that the same Indians and all other peoples, even though they are outside the faith, ... are to be able to use and enjoy this liberty and this ownership of property freely and licitly, and are not to be reduced to slavery."[107]

Like Mary of the Visitation, the Catholic Church hastened to bring the message of God's love and freedom from the shackles of sin to all peoples, even those "hitherto unknown to us." Much of the hurry was caused by the concern that Protestant Holland and England might reach these people first to teach of a salvation devoid of sacraments, saints, or popes.

Beyond protecting the liberty of indigenous peoples, Pope Paul III made another decisive move for the spread of the gospel at this dawn of the Age of Discovery by approving the Society of Jesus, with the 1540 Bull *Regimini Militantis Ecclesiae*. Founded by St. Ignatius of Loyola, this committed, educated, courageous

---

[107] Pope Paul III, encyclical *Sublimus Dei* (May 29, 1537), http://www.papalencyclicals.net/paul03/p3subli.htm.

group of young men chose to put themselves at the service of the pope in his mission of exploration and evangelization. The Jesuit missionaries went out into the new worlds, bringing Christ and His teachings to all the recently discovered areas.

One of these Jesuits, St. Francis Xavier, became a legend of missionary work, traveling to India and baptizing an estimated hundred thousand people as he went. After ministering in India and Japan, Francis Xavier died in 1552, while awaiting entry into China. Beatified in 1619 and canonized three years later, Francis Xavier inspired many artists to try to capture in paint the zeal of the missionaries and the exotic locales in which they preached.

MISSIONARIES ON CANVAS

Peter Paul Rubens was a Flemish artist who came to Rome in the Jubilee Year of 1600. His family had converted to Catholicism when he was a child, and the young painter wanted to learn the great art of Christian storytelling from the magnificent works in Rome. He returned home ready to share the monumental, dramatic style he had developed in the city that boasted the grandeur of the Roman Empire and of Michelangelo. In 1618, he produced the massive canvas of the *Miracles of Francis Xavier* for the Jesuit church in Antwerp. At 17.5 feet high, it was meant to loom large over the congregation, as if they had been transported to another world.

St. Francis, majestic in his black Jesuit habit, stands calmly as marvelous events occur with tumultuous abandon all around him. In the upper left, demonic idols crack and fall while below a man is raised from the dead. A woman baptized during a difficult delivery stands below with her newborn child, while another man rises from the dead even as grave diggers prepare his burial. On the lower right, the lame and the blind approach,

The Miracles of St. Francis Xavier by Peter Paul Rubens

looking for healing. The saint, lit from behind, points upward toward Christ's Cross of salvation and the female figure sitting on a cloud, who is the personification of faith. St. Francis draws eyes beyond himself to the Lord. Behind him, his companion carries the Gospel.

The delight Rubens evidently found in attempting to represent the different somatic features of the peoples of these new worlds is one of the greatest pleasures to viewers of the work. From the exotic topknot of the resurrected man, to the varying shades of African skin, to the Semitic traits of the official who wears his tall hat and yellow robes, the sheer variety of humanity illustrates the new look of the universal Church.

THE MISSION OF THE MAGI

To organize this massive project of global outreach, Pope Gregory XV founded the Congregation for the Propagation of the Faith (Sacra Congregatio de Propaganda Fide) in 1622 — the same year he canonized both Ignatius of Loyola and Francis Xavier. The congregation was tasked with transmitting and disseminating the Faith throughout the world and with coordinating and guiding all the Church's diverse missionary efforts.

The building housing the congregation, constructed under Pope Urban VIII, contains a stunning chapel by Borromini dedicated to the Three Magi, symbol par excellence of the Church's universal mission. Exotic kings, thinkers, and adventurers had brought their gifts to the infant Jesus. Sixteen hundred years later, the missionaries would go out to faraway lands to bring the gift of Christ.

A little museum poignantly testifies to the efforts of the missionaries and of the administration that supported them. Typeface in a myriad of languages underscores the importance of the written word in the communication of the gospel, and the memorials to martyrs who died bringing the word of God to distant lands are reminders of the powerful witness of missionaries.

Ceiling of Magi Chapel by Francesco Borromini

The amount of information lovingly collected and meticulously organized over many years makes the Propaganda Fide appear as an early *Wikipedia*, amassing and sharing information about everything from local recipes and laws to indigenous flora and fauna from all over the world.

THE WORLD IN A FOUNTAIN

The vastness of the mission and the energy of its faith was spectacularly expressed by Gian Lorenzo Bernini's Four Rivers fountain in the Piazza Navona. In 1645 Pope Innocent X had made the University of Santo Tomás in Manila the first school to receive a university charter in Asia. Three years later, he hired Bernini to design the Four Rivers fountain to express the new universality of the church under his reign.

Bernini created one of Rome's most beloved fountains as the perfect emblem for the Age of Discovery. The obelisk, of Aswan granite and inscribed with a hymn to the Roman emperor

Domitian, was found on the Via Appia. Egyptians had made obelisks as symbols of emanations from the sun god Ra; they symbolized beams of light sent from the heavens. Roman emperors brought them to the Eternal City as loot from their military victories, but then they fell and crumbled along with the empire. Bernini transformed the pagan object into a symbol of Christian illumination, raising it on a hollow base so that it appears to be descending from the skies. The dove and the olive branch, symbol of Innocent X's Pamphilj family, continued the theme of water, alluding to the covenant between God and Noah for the salvation of all mankind.

The obelisk hovers above four platforms hewn out of rough stone, upon which recline personifications of the principal rivers of the world known at the time. The Nile poses next to an expertly carved palm tree and crouching lion, its head covered because of the then-unknown source of the river. The confidence of the Age of Discovery is evident in the figure lifting the veil —they may not have found the origin of the river yet, but they are certain that they will. The Ganges, next to him, carries a long pole to allude to its navigability, but the strange sea serpent curled around it evokes the exotic animals of the east. The Danube, for Europe, sits complacently by a rearing horse, while another fanciful figure reclines almost in fear of the light streaming from above. This statue represents the Plata River between Uruguay and Argentina. The facial features show a lack of knowledge of the somatic traits of the people of South America, and the peculiar lizard-type creature indicates Bernini's unfamiliarity with local fauna. But the carefully carved coins under the hip of the figure indicate the celebrity of the wealth of the new world.

The four figures are contained within a circular basin with water flowing from the spigots around the statues to the edges — the

Fountain of the Four Rivers by Gian Lorenzo Bernini

world that contains such marvelous lands and wondrous creatures. Bernini gave the world a glorious image of Christian globalization, the light of truth, disseminated to the four corners
of the globe through the work and care of the Holy Father and
his missionaries.

Chapter 18

EMPIRICISM AND FAITH

—————————— ❖ ——————————

Today's literary onslaught decrying the Church's inability to cope with the dawn of the Age of Science, has sunk modernity into a quagmire of faith-versus-science thinking. This legacy of the Enlightenment, which believed that faith and science were incompatible, blurred the strides and struggles of the preceding Age of Discovery to accommodate the rapidly expanding knowledge of the natural world into the framework of revealed truth. Nature, subject to death and decay, was fascinating to the post-Reformation Church, but the emphasis always lay on the eternal, and the soul's share in that eternity.

The Protestants, despite the mantra of justification through faith alone, demanded constant scriptural proofs, whether of Purgatory or intercession or indulgences. Centuries of tradition and magisterial teaching on biblical revelation were no longer sufficient for them. Proof was confined to a personal understanding of Scripture, and when the Scripture did not match the Reformer's ideas, it was removed, as in the case of the books of Tobit, Judith, First and Second Maccabees, Wisdom, Sirach, and Baruch. As people grew in experience and knowledge of this world, they learned to demand proof but didn't always know how to weave discovery into the fabric of faith.

Exploration of the world fueled the development of better learning tools. Besides the printing press, this age saw the introduction of the Mercator map, the telescope, and the microscope. The first anatomical theater was built in Padua in 1594 for the study of the human body, and a few decades later Marcello Malpighi pioneered microscopic anatomy in Bologna. People gazed at the heavens and examined the world around them with greater attention than ever before. As man became better able to calculate time and measure vast distances, a new class of heroic figures rose up alongside the princes, preachers, and soldiers: university professors. Ulisse Aldrovandi, Gerardus Mercator, Galileo Galilei, Marcello Malpighi, and René Descartes all became household names in this era, their portraits painted for admiring fans.

Science became a ticket to stardom, and the adulation, condemnation, fame, and fortunes that came with it required a powerful anchor to avoid drifting off course.

Painters themselves had been treated like rock stars since the days of Leonardo da Vinci and Michelangelo. Art had become a path to international success, in which a person of little or no social status could eventually be feted in the most glamorous courts. Painters played with science—mathematical perspective, along with the camera obscura—to reveal the natural world more accurately in art. Balancing the natural and the supernatural in their images, artists were uniquely qualified to bring a moderating voice to what at times turned into polemical debate.

That the Church embraced the era of discovery is evident by the legions of missionaries sent out by the newly established Propaganda Fide. This engagement took many forms, including collecting the newest types of maps. Belgian geographer Geraldus

Mercator had developed charts for accurate global navigation in 1569 but became famous for making terrestrial globes. They became hugely popular, ranging from large (almost two feet in diameter) to the tiny "fist-size" versions he had made for the Holy Roman Emperor. Virtually every prelate owned one, as the dozens on display in modern museums attest.

MENDICANT AND MAPMAKER

On the other side of the Alps, Italy had produced its own cosmographer in the person of Ignazio Danti. A Dominican priest and a renowned mathematician, Danti was called to Rome by Pope Gregory XIII to reform the calendar, resynchronizing the human measurement of time with the movements in the heavens. The new calendar, today called the Gregorian calendar, was implemented on October 4, 1582.

At the same time, Danti was involved in another, more artistic project. The Gallery of Maps, the longest corridor of the Vatican Museums, was built under Pope Gregory XIII to feature forty panoramic maps of Italy, dividing the peninsula into its political territories and regions from the Alpine regions to the Mediterranean islands. Danti and his brother prepared the cartoons for the exceptionally accurate maps, complete with legend and scale. They were presented from an aerial perspective, like a satellite image from four hundred years ago. The maps emphasized man's ability to measure and control his geographical space. Famous battles were sketched on their respective territories and the great sixteenth-century effort to keep Islam at bay was prominently featured in the naval battle of Lepanto and the Siege of Malta. The hall underscored the Italian peninsula as a sea power, from the extensive coastal views and orientation to the little encomium for Christopher Columbus of Liguria, the

Gallery of Maps by Ignazio Danti

Genovese navigator who discovered new worlds and opened this great time of discovery and cartography.

The gallery ceiling tempered the enthusiasm for human achievement, however. Designed in tandem with the maps by Cesare Nebbia and his extensive studio, the vault features a bewildering array of decorative motifs culled from the ancient world, with pseudo-bronze reliefs, fanciful figures, and vegetation, and expanses of gilt stucco. The gaudy ornamentation was subordinated to a series of narrative scenes, each showing a miracle. These delightful images, some boasting the first landscapes in Italian painting, others rendering busy masses of figures and animals, all showed supernatural events taking place in the maps below. Several scenes involved Eucharistic miracles, such as Claire freeing besieged Assisi by holding aloft the Host, and the blood-stained corporal of the miracle of Bolsena. Others showed the remarkable Holy House of Mary in Loreto or the apparition of St. Michael the Archangel on Monte Gargano.

The entry points proclaimed conversion, with St. Paul's arrival in Italy to bring the Gospel and Constantine's establishment of the first Christian basilicas. Other panels extolled relics, such as the Shroud of Turin and the remains of John the Baptist. The most charming, however, featured religious orders, mostly Dominicans and Franciscans, involved in extraordinary events. The delightful *St. Anthony Preaching to Fish in Rimini*, pictures the serene Franciscan preaching by the shores of the Adriatic before a myriad of fish of different species. The townspeople gather in amazement, almost as startled as the viewer, astonished by the variety of sea creatures present in such a limited space.

This hall served as more than cheerful entertainment or an illustration of papal dominion; it also helped to relativize the significance of the natural sciences. Western civilization of the sixteenth century could sail the seas, map the planet, and measure time, but there were always things that could not be explained or controlled scientifically. That realm, where God makes all things possible, had manifested itself in every area of Italy, regardless of political allegiance or military might, mostly through the holy lives of the saints.

The art of portraiture took a surprising turn in the sixteenth century as university professors joined the ranks of princes, wealthy merchants, and prelates in sitting for portraits. Friends with kings and popes, the scientist-teacher enjoyed a special prestige in the post-Reformation age and these men rocketed to fame (and controversy) as men of knowledge and experience. Ulisse Aldrovandi, "the father of natural history," taught at the University of Bologna, where one of his strongest supporters

Portrait of a Botanist by Bartolomeo Passarotti

in his studies was Pope Gregory XIII, while the Medici princes sponsored Galileo Galilei.

A couple of these students and teachers of nature were immortalized by Bartolomeo Passarotti, an unconventional Bolognese painter who experimented with oil on copper, depicted fishmongers and butcher shops, and enjoyed a close friendship with Aldrovandi. Besides an allegorical portrait of the famous naturalist, in 1570 Passarotti also painted a botanist and an astronomer of the University of Bologna. The botanist stands before a table with jars and plants arrayed behind him and his notes open on the desk. The pose is that of a teacher, as the figure looks toward the viewer, gesticulating toward his work, explaining his experiments, and sharing his knowledge. The astronomer, on the other hand, is seen at night, sitting at his desk, holding his texts, but pointing toward the celestial globe; like the terrestrial globes, these were sold in vast quantities during this era. There is a figure crouched on top of the sphere, peering down, alluding to empirical observation of the heavens, as does the open window with a telescope pointed into the night sky. As tools and opportunities to study the heavens and earth increased, so did the role of scientists who could interpret the mysteries of nature.

CANVASSING THE CONTROVERSY: GALILEO

The remarkable speed with which scientific discoveries were taking place began to outpace the assumed and accumulated knowledge of the world. Tensions grew between the impatience of scientists who wanted to trademark discoveries and patent theories based on the newly acquired data, and the concerns of the Church, which, having already seen souls knocked sideways by the Protestant Reformation, wanted to assess the new information more slowly. The most famous conflict to result from this tension was that between Galileo Galilei and Pope Urban VIII, over the former's publication of *The Dialogue Concerning the Two Chief World Systems* in 1632. A rock-star scientist, Galileo had discovered moons around Jupiter, challenged the Aristotelian concepts of bodies in motion, and invented the thermometer.

Portrait of an Astronomer by Bartolomeo Passarotti

Well aware of his status, he often ruffled feathers, whether of the Grand Duchess of Lorraine, his Medici proctors, the Jesuits, and eventually even his friend Pope Urban VIII.

His work attracted many admirers, such as the Oratorian Cesare Baronio, who reputedly told the young astronomer, "The Holy Spirit's intention is to teach us how to go to Heaven, and not how the heavens go."[108] While still a cardinal, Pope Urban VIII had been a loyal supporter, signing his correspondence to Galileo, "Your affectionate brother."[109]

Galileo's *Dialogue* and the subsequent trial was in many ways a comedy of errors featuring an offended pope, jealous courtiers, half-truths, and rival scientists, and, most importantly, Galileo's lack of proof to substantiate the assertion—without the required hypothetical phrasing —that the earth revolved around the sun. This sad story broke up friendships and embarrassed many people who had been loyal supporters of Galileo. Meanwhile, one prominent family tried to evaluate what had happened through a work of art.

Cardinals Virgilio and Bernardino Spada were brothers from Bologna whose fortunes had risen under Pope Urban VIII. As legate to Bologna, Bernardino enjoyed being at the nerve center of modern learning, and as an Oratorian, Virgilio, together with Baronio, had befriended Galileo and sponsored him in the Lynx-Eyed Society— the science club founded by another erudite cardinal, Federico Cesi. The brothers were disgraced by Galileo's trial and condemnation and eventually retreated into a quiet life sponsoring art. Virgilio Spada had befriended a Sienese painter, Niccolò Tornioli, who had produced several canvases for the brothers, but the most personal would be the Spada's assessment of the "Galileo Affair" in *The Astronomers*. Painted shortly after the scientist's death in 1642, Tornioli's work captured the tensions that the clash between the pope and his friend the astronomer had brought to the surface.

[108] William R. Shea and Mariano Artigas, *Galileo in Rome: The Rise and Fall of a Troublesome Genius* (Oxford: Oxford University Press, 2003), 48.

[109] Ibid.

The Astronomers by Niccolò Tornioli

The painting feels cramped, as figures crowd the small space. They appear ready to burst from the canvas, much as the debate over heliocentricity and the role of science versus Scripture had erupted from the classroom and chapels into everyday life. The shadows in the work are oppressive, filling the space and overwhelming the actors. This pervasive darkness evokes the lack of clarity in this situation; the empirical theories lack proof, while the textual tradition was contradicted by observation.

On the left, the old school of thought gathers around Ptolemy, who, in the second century, had developed the working explanation of planetary movement, and Aristotle, whose philosophy, which also included physics, had entered the capillaries of the development of Catholic doctrine. The Greek is an older man clutching his book as it seems to slide out of his grasp, while the Roman is portrayed as a soldier, an allusion to Ptolemy Soter, general of Alexander the Great. A young student gazes in admiration toward the pair, his lifted finger pointing to the peripatetic philosopher as the ultimate authority. Another man juts in, gesticulating energetically amid the dignified assembly. He is Nicholas Copernicus, the sixteenth-century astronomer and cleric who had first broached the heliocentric theory in writing, albeit in a hypothetical fashion. Copernicus interrupts the thinkers by pointing dramatically to the sky. Aristotle lays a restraining hand on the Polish astronomer to invite him to reflect before leaping to conclusions, but Copernicus is animated by what his eyes have seen.

The new school of astronomy is busily at work on the right side of the painting. They study nature, not texts. The woman, the personification of philosophy, shows a young student how to use a telescope with a sextant, and he directs his gaze toward the terrestrial globe. People crowd in to see this innovative technology while behind them, a mysterious yet inviting expanse of starry sky opens. This is a new world, with bold new discoveries to be made. A shadowy figure emerges from the background, surveying the excitement from a distance. This is Galileo, the friend and protégé of the Spadas, who is now in the heavens, surveying the continuation of his work from afar.

THE DECEIT OF THE SENSES

The debate between the traditional understanding of the natural world and the sometimes-contradictory information brought by empirical data in some ways reflected the experience of the Protestant Reformation itself. Ancient scriptural interpretation was undermined by novel explanations, which hacked away at the foundations of belief in the sacraments, the saints, and the Magisterium. Sensory knowledge was certainly here to stay, but how to make the faithful aware of its limitations?

The Jesuits produced one of the most provocative, yet delightful, responses to this dilemma with the aid of art. In 1622, St. Ignatius was canonized, and work commenced on a new Roman church in his honor. The construction, designed by Jesuit Orazio Grassi, lagged for decades due to financial problems and was still unfinished at the time of Galileo's death. In 1650, the work was complete, but the church lacked a dome, by now a standard feature of the churches of the Catholic Restoration. This humiliating and aesthetically distressing situation provided the Jesuits with a chance to make a marvelous point in the age of empiricism.

In 1685, a Jesuit lay brother and artist, Andrea Pozzo, was commissioned to decorate the church. The crossing had left space for a dome, but it had never been constructed. Pozzo creatively filled the gap by painting a flat canvas with an illusionistic cupola and pulling it into place. An astounding display of the power of perspective painting, the work appeared to rise in a hemispherical vault, complete with coffers and windows that seemed to let in light. From the threshold to the crossing, the viewer would see what looked to be a three-dimensional dome, an illusion that would work until he reached a yellow stone dot on the floor exactly at the transept.

This marked the point where churches often had rood screens before the Protestant Reformation. New churches, like Sant'Ignazio, not only had no screens, but also placed the tabernacle squarely on the altar. As the faithful moved out of the nave toward the sanctuary and the space of the tabernacle, the illusion began to fade, the dome appearing to melt into a jumble of disorganized shapes. This reflected no deficiency on the part of Pozzo, but it was a challenge to the viewer, who had been lured to this point with the delight of a trompe l'oeil dome. As the beholder realized that his senses had fooled him into believing he was looking at a three-dimensional dome, he had to ask himself if his senses could also be mistaken when they told him that the bread and wine of the Eucharist were merely matter.

After a long period of struggle, the Church found a way to delight and challenge the faithful during this empirical age, to make them reflect pleasurably without antagonistic debate.

Chapter 19

THE BLOOD OF THE MARTYRS IS THE SEED OF THE CHURCH

---- ❧ ----

Martin Luther was a young pilgrim to Rome in 1510, climbing the steps of the Holy Stairs next to the Cathedral of St. John Lateran, when he experienced his life-changing revelation that "the just shall live by faith." Standing before the twenty-eight steps thought to be those that Christ climbed to be judged by Pontius Pilate, with pilgrims all around him ascending on their knees, Luther came to reject the relics, practices, and sites connected with the Roman Catholic Church. And so began Luther's battle over the apostolic tradition.

Against the Catholic claim of the rootlessness of Protestant thought, Luther said his teaching was "not a novel invention of ours but the very ancient, approved teaching of the apostles brought to light again."[110] The Protestants sought not "to have anything new in Christendom" but instead struggled "to hold to the ancient: that which Christ and the apostles have left behind them and have given to us."[111] They claimed that this

[110] *Luther's Works on CD-ROM*, vol. 24, 368.
[111] Ibid.

teaching had been "obscured by the pope with human doctrine, aye, decked out in dust and spider webs and all sorts of vermin, and flung and trodden into the mud besides, we have by God's grace brought it out again ... to the light of day."[112]

So, who had the claim to tradition? Which teaching had the martyrs died for? What role did relics play: were they a testimony to ancient history, or were they, as John Calvin wrote in his *Treatise on Relics*, an "abomination"?

WITNESSES FROM THE ROMAN SOIL

An astonishing find on the Via Salaria on May 31, 1578, armed the Church with a potent response. Some workmen accidentally discovered the entrance to one of the Christian catacombs, an underground burial site with thousands of tombs. These mass graves, lost since the ninth century, were decorated with hundreds of paintings, witnesses to the early Christian Church and her beliefs.

Antonio Bosio, a young lawyer-turned-archaeologist who was close to Philip Neri's new congregation, the Oratorians, took it upon himself to explore these underground sites. He was dubbed the "Christopher Columbus of Underground Rome," and his lifetime of work was crowned with the publication, three years after his death in 1629, of *Roma Sotterranea Cristiana*: a guide to the Roman catacombs, complete with illustrations.

Bosio's first catacomb visit brought him to the cemetery of Domitilla, where he saw (and signed) an image of Christ transmitting His teaching to the apostles with St. Peter seated in the direct line of His hand. Bosio also identified congested spaces where the graves of the faithful were clustered around the tombs

---

[112] Ibid.

of martyrs, in the hopes of intercession on the Day of Judgment. These images provided powerful witness to a Catholic tradition of scriptural interpretation, including pictures taken from the stories of Susanna in the book of Daniel, which had been expunged from the Protestant Bible.

St. Cecilia Recovers Her Voice

The most exciting discovery, however, took place in 1599, on the eve of the great Jubilee Year of 1600, when the incorrupt body of St. Cecilia was found in what had been her home in Trastevere. Executed in the third century, St. Cecilia, a virgin martyr, was originally interred in the catacomb of St. Callistus. In 821, Pope Paschal had removed her incorrupt body from the catacombs, which were about to be closed and sealed. He placed it in a crypt in the church he was building in her honor, in the Trastevere neighborhood of Rome. In 1599, a commission opened the tomb and found her body intact.

The youthful artist Stefano Maderno was immediately commissioned to make a sculpture of this saint who testified to the virtue of chastity in an age when licentiousness reigned, who gave away her considerable material wealth in an era of luxury, and who worked in close collaboration with Pope Urban I to convert her husband and brother-in-law to the true faith. Cardinal Paolo Emilio Sfondrato (also a close friend of Philip Neri) commissioned the work and arranged its placement under the main altar of the church.

The graceful statue, modeled on her actual body, shows a sleeping Cecilia inside a space identical to that of her tomb. No gritty Caravaggio-style drama or affected Mannerist poses here: the fluid lines convey serenity. Only upon closer inspection does the sharply turned head and the thin slice mark on her neck

Martyrdom of St. Cecilia by Stefano Maderno

reveal the brutality of her murder. Her hands rest close to the viewer, clasped in the age-old gesture of belief in the Trinity (three fingers extended) and in Christ's dual nature as God and man (the open finger and thumb on her left hand). The marble is softly polished to allow a gentle glow to illuminate her body from the darkness of the tomb.

SURROUND-SOUND MARTYRDOM

Alongside the rediscovery of the tombs and bodies of the martyrs, the stories of their passions were undergoing an overhaul by Oratorian cardinal Cesare Baronio. After writing a history of the Roman Church at the request of Philip Neri, Baronio turned his attention to the Roman martyrology, examining the lives of saints and martyrs in light of the literary, scriptural, and archaeological evidence.

The savage nature of the Roman persecutions grew in relevance as the Reformation devolved into violence throughout Europe. Thomas More's beheading and the hanging of the nineteen Martyrs of Gorkum seemed tame compared to the drawing and quartering of Edmund Campion and the horrific tortures that awaited the missionaries in North America or in Japan. The excavations of the thousands of subterranean graves nestled side by side bore quiet witness to the fact that although many in the early Christian community in Rome had died humiliating, painful, and unjust deaths, they had found peace in Christ.

The brutality of the martyrs' deaths became fodder for many church frescoes, especially those where young missionaries were to be trained: priests who would go out to the hostile lands and often die gruesomely themselves as they witnessed to the Faith. The most powerful example is the martyrdom cycle in the Church of San Stefano Rotondo (St. Stephen in the Round), frescoed by Pomerancio in 1583 for the German-speaking Jesuits who would be sent back to Germany to try to convert the Protestants back to the true Faith.

Starting with St. Stephen himself, thirty-four large panels encircle the viewer, showing the varied and violent deaths of the martyrs. From being thrown to the beasts, to being hacked to

Frescoes in San Stefano Rotondo

death with machetes, or boiled in oil, or crushed by giant blocks of stone, Christians had known the gamut of human cruelty. These images graphically recalled what the early commitment to the Faith looked like in the face of persecution by the powerful Roman Empire.

These relics, frescoes, and other testimonies were housed in churches, some of them ancient, with roots going back to the time of Sts. Peter and Paul. The Catholic Church realized that even more than peering at the tombs or looking at pictures, standing in a space where the Eucharist had been celebrated for fifteen hundred years expressed the continuity of the ancient teaching better than anything else.

Prelates were enlisted to breathe new life into the oldest churches: Cardinal Baronio rebuilt the ancient house church of Sts. Nereus and Achilleus using vivid martyrdom imagery; St. Charles Borromeo redesigned St. Praxedes, adding special galleries where the most important relics could be displayed. He gave personal witness as well, spending nights in prayer in the *confessio* under the altar, amid the relics of the martyrs taken from the catacombs. Cardinal Enrico Caetani remodeled the fourth-century Church of Santa Pudenziana, home of the sisters Praxedes and Pudenziana, where St. Peter had lived when he first arrived in Rome. Cardinal Caetani commissioned Giovanni Paolo Rossetti to paint these sisters (who were baptized by St. Peter) as they collected in a well the precious relics of the blood shed by the first witnesses to the Faith in Rome.

Laypeople, albeit unlikely to be tested for their Faith in Catholic Rome, or recruited as foreign missionaries, tried to participate in the spirit of sacrifice and witness. Jubilee Year 1575 had seen a remarkable resurgence of lay confraternities in Italy, particularly in Rome.

*Sts. Praxedes and Pudenziana Collecting the Blood
of the Martyrs* by Giovanni Paolo Rossetti

SHARING IN THE SUFFERING OF THE MARTYRS

Confraternities were associations of the faithful, supervised by an ecclesiastical authority, that engaged in works of piety or charity. As the Protestants downplayed the importance of works in salvation, Catholic confraternities grew in number and gained increasing Church support. The principal activities of the sodalities involved corporal acts of mercy: some buried the dead; others took care of prisoners or tended to the poor. The brothers also carried out public acts of penance, such as processions including self-flagellation during Holy Week. While these men (and women) could not achieve the crown of martyrdom, they labored to emulate Christ as closely as possible in His self-giving and in His suffering.

The oldest lay brotherhood in Rome dated back to the thirteenth century. Named for the banners its members carried in processions, the Confraternity of the Gonfalone was elevated by Pope Gregory XIII in 1579 to the prestigious rank of archconfraternity. Their tasks expanded to include services such as ransoming prisoners captured by Islamic pirates and accompanying a paroled prisoner on his return to society.

Cardinal Alessandro Farnese, the patron of the Jesuits, also served as cardinal protector of the confraternity. From 1568 to 1575, while he was funding the Church of the Gesù, Cardinal Farnese commissioned a series of large frescoes to envelope the walls of the confraternity's main meeting space. The seven artists chosen to execute the scenes of Christ's Passion were the most promising painters of the first generation of post-Tridentine art.

The confraternity members spent Holy Week in special penitential activities. They staged Stations of the Cross, gave alms to the poor and the sick, and marched through the streets barefoot while scourging their backs. Their robes were designed to allow their backs to be bared, but their heads were covered so as to avoid advertisement of personal piety.

As they prepared to go out and suffer pain and perform works, they prayed in this frescoed space, with the example of Christ's suffering all around them. The first scene was painted by Bettoja, a favorite of the cardinal, and showed Christ's Palm Sunday procession. Crowds press in adoringly as Jesus emerges on a donkey; the palms wave, and people prostrate themselves before Him. The bright busyness of the frescoes reminded the brothers that the glories of this world are transient, and the admiration of men is fickle. Marcantonio dal Forno painted the haunting *Arrest of Christ*, anticipating Caravaggio's dramatic lighting effects by twenty years.

The most striking work, entrusted to Federico Zuccari, was the *Flagellation of Christ*, which held special meaning for the confraternity as flagellants. The scene unfolds inside a Roman arch, where three men, faces contorted to the point of caricature, are energetically preparing to strike Jesus with bundled rods, similar to those used by the confraternity. Christ, luminous and as yet unbloodied, bows under the weight of the first blow. One Roman poses on the left, staring insolently at the viewer as a crowd gathers on the balcony above, jeering and pointing. Another group of soldiers, placed surprisingly low in the frame, essentially at the eye level of the viewer, gesticulate toward the spectacle, but one soldier, elbow jutting out of the pictorial space, calmly stares at the beholder, hand on his chin as he waits with the crown of thorns. Jesus' example of self-sacrifice seems beyond reach for the viewer confined to the cruel world of men. The brothers of the confraternity, however, with their charitable acts and harsh self-mortification, attempted to offer their lives to Christ, even if martyrdom was not their destiny.

The Flagellation by Federico Zuccari

As home to thousands of martyrs over hundreds of years, Rome's claim to the authentic tradition of Christ and the apostles was already strong, but the Catholic Restoration sought to reinforce this ancient memory. Efforts to excavate, rebuild, and decorate the most ancient spaces of the Faith formed a persuasive argument for the deep roots of Catholic Rome, as did the public witness of the many Roman confraternities. "The blood of the martyrs is the seed of the Church" wrote Tertullian in 197, defying the Imperial persecutions.[113] Thirteen hundred years later, Rome proudly reclaimed that tradition in her art, her architecture, and her citizens.

---

[113] Tertullian, *Apologeticum*, Tertullian Project, http://www.tertullian.org/works/apologeticum.htm.

Chapter 20

THE DIGNITY OF WOMEN IN
THE CATHOLIC RESTORATION

The first phase of the Reformation was not particularly good to women, despite the fact that many Protestant churches would later champion women's ordination. The elimination of Mary's role as supreme intercessor, the abolition of women's religious orders (indeed, Martin Luther married a nun), and the rejection of the female martyrs of the Paleo-Christian era as mere legends and fantasies left women of the age without role models or guides in the complicated waters of late-Renaissance society. Luther freed women from the confines of religious life, only to confine their actions and authority to the hearth.

Furthermore, several Protestant leaders saw women as unfit for any kind of leadership. John Calvin wrote that women ought to be subject to men for two reasons, "because not only did God enact this law at the beginning, but He also inflicted it as a punishment on the woman."[114] German painter Lucas Cranach the Elder, a

[114] John Calvin, *Commentaries on St. Paul's Epistles to Timothy, Titus and Philemon* (Altenmünster, Germany: Jazzybee Verlag, 2012), 67.

close friend of Luther, depicted women as sly, provocative, and simpering. They invariably sported a sidelong glance—whether when offering Adam the forbidden fruit or seducing a foolish old husband. These ideas were certainly not limited to the Reformers, but the Protestants lacked a repertoire of beautiful, holy women to temper the harsher view of women as wily temptresses or to develop a more nuanced appreciation for the role of women.

The Catholic Church had the advantage of centuries of Marian veneration and a liturgical calendar filled with heroic, holy women, and she also knew, much like advertisers today, that nothing sells better than a beautiful woman. Women in the Church found a new impetus in the Counter-Reformation, especially in the extraordinary lives of people such as St. Teresa of Avila, who reformed the Carmelite Order and wrote powerfully about her experiences, or the extraordinary Vicaress Pernette de Montluel of the Poor Clares, who courageously contested the Reformers in Geneva as recorded in Jeanne de Jussie's *The Short Chronicle*.

Depictions of women—often created by women—flourished in this age, not only as biblical heroines, but also as models of new ways in which women could use their unique gifts to spread the gospel. Images of formidable Old Testament women proliferated in the Counter-Reformation, from Judith slaying Holofernes to Susanna defying the lecherous elders, while Mary Magdalene became the model par excellence of conversion and repentance. The rediscovery of the bodies of St. Cecilia and St. Agnes in the newly excavated catacombs reignited devotion to the bravery of the virgin martyrs.

CATHERINE OF ALEXANDRIA

Devotion to St. Catherine of Alexandria, however, enjoyed a particularly significant renewal during this period.

This saint who lived in the third and fourth centuries was a well-educated Christian aristocrat who was sent as an envoy to the Roman emperor to protest the persecution of the Church. Beautiful as well as wise, Catherine suffered under Emperor Maxentius's attempts first to seduce her, offering her the role of "second wife," and then, upon her refusal, to break her through a grueling interrogation before fifty of his most erudite philosophers. Catherine converted them all with her reasoned arguments for the truth of Christianity and was thereupon sentenced to death. The spiked wheel devised for her torture (ubiquitous in her iconography and lending its name to a type of fireworks) was destroyed by angels before it could harm her, so Catherine was swiftly beheaded and her body carried off by angels to Mount Sinai.

Counter-Reformation artists were inundated with commissions for images of this saint, the patroness of philosophy. Where Luther had claimed that "no gown worse becomes a woman than the desire to be wise,"[115] this lovely woman had gained Heaven not only for herself but for all seekers of truth who came into contact with her. Caravaggio painted her in contemporary dress, with a fair but familiar face, as if one might run into this heroic paragon of wisdom on the street. The centuries-old saint was given a new look for the modern age that had disdained reason and sought salvation through faith alone.

Catherine became the poster child for the art of philosophy. Though the chronicles recounting her life were riddled with inaccuracies and lacking in evidence, Cesare Baronio, the cardinal Pope Clement VIII entrusted to purge the martyrology of saints whose lives could be held up to Protestant ridicule as mere

---

[115] *The Table Talk of Martin Luther* (London: George Bell, 1902), 367.

myth or legend, left her memorial in the breviary as a prominent feast. As Luther denigrated philosophy, Aristotle, and St. Thomas Aquinas, so the Catholic Church responded by putting forth a lovely woman of privilege who persuaded not with her physical or material attractions but with her utter command of reason and truth.

Catherine also became the front woman for religious sisters. The Reformers closed convents, casting women adrift into the world. In rejecting the emperor's suit, Catherine claimed, "Christ has taken me to Himself as a bride; I have joined myself to Him as a bride in an indissoluble bond." This mystical marriage, never mentioned in her acts, became a preferred subject of the Counter-Reformation.

Annibale Carracci painted a particularly cherished version of Catherine in 1587 for the wealthy Farnese family. Although many artists tackled the subject, including Guercino, Ludovico Carracci, Albani, and Cavorozzi, Annibale added a romantic flourish, as charming as any love story, perfect for a devotional piece intended for the young, beautiful, privileged women of this aristocratic family. Like Romeo and Juliet, wedded at night, this intimate marriage emerges as light out of darkness. Soft blush and rose tones frame the radiant wedding party. Catherine, regally dressed in gold and mulberry, gazes downward like a modest bride as she proffers her long elegant fingers toward Christ. The luminous child gently caresses her hand while embracing His mother, uniting the virgin princess and the Blessed Virgin. The angel drawing the betrothed together forms a shimmering golden backdrop for the scene, but the red sashes that cross his chest allude to the fact that this love, sealed today with a ring, will be consummated in blood when she follows Christ to martyrdom. Try as they might, neither Shakespeare nor Hollywood has ever produced a love story as compelling as this.

The Mystical Marriage of Saint Catherine by Annibale Carracci

During the Catholic Restoration, women were not only exalted after their death as saints but were allowed room to lead in society and Church institutions. Beyond the stateswomen such as Mary Tudor of England and Mary of Scots, Catherine de' Medici, and Jeanne d'Albret, St. Angela Merici founded the Ursulines to offer serious Christian education for girls and young women, Victoria Colonna composed renowned poetry and debated theology, and the art world produced its first celebrated female painters.

On one hand, technological advances had opened the door for women painters. Oil painting permitted women to work alone (not with a team of male fresco artists) in an inexpensive, slow-drying medium. Simultaneously, the Catholic Church was looking for new ways to evangelize through art and was unafraid to give women a chance. Sofonisba Anguissola, Elisabetta Sirani, and Artemisia Gentileschi all had very successful careers working for both private and ecclesiastical patrons, but it was Lavinia Fontana who would burst the canvas ceiling when she was commissioned to produce the first Italian altarpiece to be painted by a woman in her native Bologna.

Her patron was none other than the powerful archbishop Gabriele Paleotti, who had recently published the *Discourses on Sacred and Profane Images* in 1582. As an expert in art and decorum, this cardinal, friend to St. Charles Borromeo, catapulted Lavinia's career to stratospheric success.

Her first altarpiece was *Christ in the House of Mary and Martha*, executed in 1580, but her style soon matured, and she was asked to produce two altarpieces in the most male-dominated art town in Italy: Rome. Her work for St. Paul Outside the Walls is lost, but her St. Hyacinth is still visible in its chapel in the Church of Santa Sabina. Her most prestigious commission (which earned her as much as a Caravaggio work) was for Phillip II of Spain, who had heard about this remarkable woman and requested *The Sleeping Christ Child*. At the height of her career in 1607, she painted a daring, beautiful version of the Samaritan Woman at the Well.

The composition is startling in its departure from most contemporary versions, which portrayed a seated Jesus, at the same height as the woman. Lavinia's Samaritan is tall, arresting and swathed in her golden robe, and she commands attention. She leans toward Jesus, who, resting His head on His hand, looks lovingly up toward her. It appears that He enjoys nothing more than being in her presence. She looks intrigued, curious, intelligent. The words He is speaking to her are not what she usually hears at this well. He admires her, sees her beauty, but not the earthy seductiveness that has brought her five husbands. Rather, he gazes at the woman whose witness will help bring about the conversion of her village. The empty jar of water, the pretext for this great moment of "empowerment," stands between them: she will go, no longer thirsty for the transient pleasures of life but sated with the waters of truth and purpose.

In the distance, so as not to disturb the intimacy of the scene, two apostles stand with their arms akimbo, shocked to see the Master in conversation with this woman. Lavinia's stunning female figure suggests that the apostles are taken aback not so much by her nationality and the traditional enmity between Samaritans and Jews, but by the Rabbi engaged in conversation with a beautiful and evidently seductive woman. She is beguiling in her sheer gown, revealing her lower leg, a corset emphasizing her small waist and voluptuous breasts, in turn highlighted with a red sash, and her golden hair escaping in soft tendrils around her face and neck. This is a woman who would have turned every village eye. But her encounter with Jesus transforms the purpose of her charm, intelligence, and boldness; the heavy rope hanging between them is a symbol of penitence. As she faces her sins under the loving gaze of Christ, she in turn becomes an effective force for evangelization. Women with

Christ and the Woman of Samaria by Lavinia Fontana

pasts, women who are searching, women who ask questions are not only welcome, but admired in this age.

Famously beautiful herself, Lavinia was happily married to Paolo Zappi, with whom she had eleven children—and who occasionally painted backgrounds for her when she was over-whelmed with work. Lavinia's life, career, and artistic vision offered women a role model that resonates beyond the sixteenth century to today—material success, happy marriage, and deep faith: she was a Catholic model of feminine genius.

THE TRIALS OF ARTEMISIA

On the other end of the spectrum, Artemisia Gentileschi's life was rocked by scandal from her rape trial at age seventeen to her later infidelities. Daughter of one of Caravaggio's closest companions, Orazio Gentileschi, Artemisia was caught in the humiliation of a public court case when her father accused one of his associates, Agostino Tassi, of raping her. Bundled off to Florence with her hastily arranged marriage to a modest Floren-tine painter, it seemed that her career might be over before it began. Yet in this age of conversion, her talents helped her to find an important role despite her changed circumstances. She was hugely successful as a painter and, with the sponsorship of Galileo Galilei, became the first woman to be inducted into the Florentine art academy. Artemisia brought a unique vision to all her works, many of which, following in the footsteps of Caravaggio, were gruesomely violent, but she also reinterpreted the Madonna and Child as perhaps only a woman could.

An obviously successful motif, she repeated the theme often, but the version in the gallery of Virgilio and Bernardino Spada is undoubtedly the most powerful. Mary is seated on a low stool with Jesus on her lap, and the only indication of the otherworldly holiness of the pair is the translucent sliver of halo around the head of the Virgin. Mary's blue robe, symbolic of grace, is slipped around her waist, but she is wrapped in the rose color of mortal-ity. The Child stretched along her lap reveals the exceptional

Madonna and Child by Artemisia Gentileschi

drawing ability of this young woman. His plump thigh is revealed up to the thin cloth clasped around His chest. This intimate moment of feeding, this private act between Mother and Son, is presented without backdrop or distraction; they focus only on each other, and the viewer focuses only on them. The Blessed Mother's eyes are closed, a first in art. Painters have depicted Mary gazing downward, outward, or upward, but Artemisia chose to present Mary's engagement in a completely novel fashion. Instead of using the sense of sight, Mary experiences the presence of her Son with her other senses. The warmth of His hand, the weight of His body, the scent of His flaxen hair, the sound of His breathing—the viewer imagines the scene through all the senses, as counseled by St. Ignatius of Loyola in his *Spiritual Exercises*. Artemisia, a young mother herself, shared the wonder of motherhood with her viewers, using the language of her empirical age.

The Catholic Restoration was an amazing age for women, and whether in art or in holiness, women found open roads and encouragement to forge their unique paths in this life with the promise of being equally exalted in the next.

Chapter 21

THE WAR ON SIN

＊

There was one important area of convergence between sixteenth-century Reformers and the Catholic Church: neither one ever denied the existence of sin. Sin was omnipresent, and humanity was swept along in a deluge of temptations and faults that constantly threatened to separate it from God. The bone of contention lay in how to swim against the tides of evil. Protestants clung to salvation by faith alone, exalting Christ's redemptive sacrifice as the source of all salvation while holding faith to be the believer's sole means of accessing unmerited grace. The Catholic Church, meanwhile, always affirming the centrality of Christ's redemption, also preached the necessity of human cooperation with divine grace and the necessity to combat sin every day. This disagreement was so bitter that it threatened to submerge everyone caught in its undertow.

St. Ignatius of Loyola plunged into the realm of spiritual combat with his *Spiritual Exercises*, teaching thousands how to face the reality of sin and to battle its effect in their lives. His spirituality would help shape a century of dramatic imagery that vividly confronted the faithful about how virtue conquers vice and incited Catholics to wage war on sin.

Archangel Michael by Guido Reni

The Ease of Angels

Leading the charge are the angels, explored in a previous chapter, who possess a superhuman capacity to combat sin without ever getting a hair out of place. As debonair as Ian Fleming's 007, Michael the Archangel, especially in Guido Reni's oft-imitated 1635 painting, treads on Satan without a spot of sweat, a dent in his cool blue armor, or a furrow in his porcelain brow. This vision of grace, undisturbed by worldly desires, depicts an easy win for the angel. Satan is suffused with the russet shade of passion and earthiness, clawing and grimacing as he struggles. The angel, ethereal and luminous, places a weightless foot on the head of the demon, and victory is assured.

But what about mere mortals—what does battling evil in daily life look like? Rarely pretty. St. Ignatius invited the world to an examination of conscience—holding up a mirror to the soul to examine the sag here and the blemish there—or as Ignatius more brutally put it, to "look upon all the corruption and foulness of my body."[116]

Contrast the elegant ease of Reni's Michael the Archangel with Niccolò Tornioli's *Cain and Abel*—what a change sin hath wrought in man! In this close-up depiction of history's first murder, Cain, engulfed in shadow, dominates the canvas as he deals the fatal blow to his brother. Abel, helpless, lies curled in the fetal position like a newborn baby. The composition follows the trajectory of Cain's strike, leading the eye from the rough club to the tumble of chestnut curls, to the pool of blood trickling toward the edge of the canvas. Abel remains beautiful in form and luminosity, but Cain is transformed. His body grows brutish, and wickedness distorts his face. He appears as feral as the pelt looped around his

[116] *Spiritual Exercises*, 66.

Cain and Abel by Niccolò Tornioli

body. In an age where Catholics and Protestants, all brothers in Christ, fought and killed each other, art held up a mirror to the ugliness of hate, envy, and violence.

Sin as Ease

Sin, however, has many guises, of which murderous violence is but one. Pleasure, too, has its perils. Legend has it that the only book in St. Ignatius's chamber at the time of his death was Thomas à Kempis's *Imitation of Christ*, a guidebook for strengthening the spirit by turning away from vanities, whether riches or bodily desires. In this era, scenes of failed seduction began to proliferate in art, allowing the enticing nature of painting to expose the challenges of resisting disordered desires. Lust-driven old men tormenting the chaste Susanna and the pagan Lucrezia choosing death over dishonor were depicted by Rome's finest artists, the scenes often shown in disquieting proximity to the viewer. The artistic preoccupation with virtuous temperance adorned everything from altars to boudoirs.

The Bolognese artist Carlo Cignani, student of the prestigious Carracci academy, developed a fascination with the subject of Joseph and Potiphar's wife — returning to it over and over again. Developing the compositions of his teachers, he intensified the intimacy of the struggle between virtuous Joseph and the seductive woman who remains unnamed in the Bible. Cignani worked in the later seventeenth century when softer brush strokes and pastel colors contributed to an idyllic atmosphere in art. A mood of languid enticement hangs over the scene.

The pretty young woman envelops Joseph in her voluptuous flesh with her red robe waving like a cape before a bull. They are entwined in the confined space of the canvas, and she is alluring, warm, desirable. Joseph must turn away from the inviting glow, toward the shadows and embrace the subsequent false accusations that his rejection will bring. Joseph holds up his hand in rejection of sin while looking to Heaven for help to resist temptation. Cignani underscored the need for prayer and

Joseph and Potiphar's Wife by Carlo Cignani

divine assistance, especially when sin appears more like a warm embrace than a slap in the Lord's face.

FACING EVIL WITH SWORDS DRAWN:
CARAVAGGIO AND ARTEMISIA

While God gives aid to those who ask it, human struggles against sin are struggles nonetheless, and art was recruited to illustrate the messiness of moral combat. After all, good exercise works up a sweat. Few knew this better than Caravaggio and Artemisia Gentileschi, two public sinners and painters who engaged in plenty of spiritual (and sometimes physical) wrestling, but their struggles produced works of art that would guide many others through the dark trenches toward holiness.

Both artists worked on the most popular biblical story of virtue conquering vice: that of Judith and Holofernes—a story missing from the Protestant biblical canon. The subject had been popular in art from the Renaissance era, when she had been portrayed by everyone from Botticelli to Donatello, but Caravaggio, painting in 1598, added a startling innovation—a much more immediate vision of the honorable widow conquering the decadent soldier. For Caravaggio, a man who bounced in and out of Roman jails on account of his violent temper, the image of struggling with inner darkness resonated deeply in his art.

A red curtain rises on the left, a signal for the viewer to pay attention to the scene. Judith's heavy sword is almost through the neck of the shocked general, who clutches the bedsheets in a final paroxysm of death. Surprised in the depths of his sin, he grimaces as the light of life leaves his eyes. Beautiful Judith arches her body away from the bloody mess, her brow furrowed in distaste. There is no enjoyment in this victory, no personal pleasure for her, just the fulfillment of a dangerous duty.

None of Holofernes's blood spills on her elegant dress, and she remains pure despite the deadly combat, bathed in bright light to illustrate the holy nature of her actions. By contrast, her eager maid gazes hungrily at the scene from the wings, two-dimensional and without complexity or nuance. Reveling in the retribution dealt to the evil general, she avidly watches the deed. Despite Judith's aversion to her task, her determination is evident in her locked arms, which counteract the broad sweep of

Judith Beheading Holofernes by Caravaggio

her pristine dress away from the spectacle. This was hard work, unpleasant work, but the work of the Lord nonetheless.

A few years later, Artemisia Gentileschi wrestled with the same subject, her painting clearly influenced by that of Caravaggio. She would return to the subject of Judith and Holofernes seven times during her life, but most intensely in 1612 (the year of her famous rape trial) and again in 1620, the year she would resettle in Rome. Her promising career in Florence had stalled on account of her infidelities with a Florentine nobleman, which had become public knowledge. Artemisia loved beautiful things and enjoyed the attentions of wealthy Francesco Maria Maringhi; she understood the difficulty of battling sinful desire. Artemisia's Judith is no shy sylph pulling away from this murder. She wrestles, blood-spattered, with the figure on the bed. Artemisia used the same motif of the locked arms that Caravaggio had employed to illustrate determination, but this image added the body weight of both women to subdue their enemy. One of Judith's hands grasps blood-soaked hair, but the other wields the sword vertically, recalling the Cross of Christ.

She is assisted by her maid, a lovely nod to female solidarity and companionship in the clash against sin and darkness. A draftswoman superior to Caravaggio, Artemisia showed the extended body on the bed, the bared legs and rumpled sheets implying the seduction Holofernes had planned for Judith. The young heroine wears a silk dress and boasts fine jewels, things

Judith Beheading Holofernes by Artemisia Gentileschi

that Artemisia herself enjoyed, but the beautiful things are be-
smirched by the blood of the evil general. The viewer stands at
the foot of the bed, the blood-stained mattress bowed toward
him, the point of the sword before his eyes. In Artemisia's view,
there is no sitting on the sidelines for the war on sin; everyone
must either fight or wait to be felled by the enemy.

The Church of the Catholic Restoration urged the faithful
actively to resist disordered desires, to be vigilant and prayerful,
lest one lose the prize of Heaven. For the members of the Church
Militant, fighting sin within and without is not as easy as it is for
the archangels; it often involves grime, dirt, and blood. There
is suffering, loss, and sacrifice, and at times the holy task is the
distasteful one. In this era, holiness was presented as a life-or-
death struggle for the immortal soul, with heroic examples of
success and tragic figures of failure. Never, during the Catholic
Restoration, was this combat downplayed as a casual task that
one can accomplish alone; thus, one looked to Christ, Mary, the
angels, intercessors, and even friends for help. This community of
combatants, brothers and sisters in arms against sin, hoped that
they would one day enjoy victory, together, in Heaven.

END GAME

The Catholic Church always perceived the battles and trials of this world in light of the bodily resurrection on the Last Day. Each life is a precious work of art, shaped, chiseled, molded, and colored to present to Jesus at the Final Judgment. Catholics work all their lives so that death might not be an end but a transition, with a desire for the smoothest transition possible from here to Heaven.

To keep the end game in sight, the Church commissioned constant reminders of human mortality in art: ubiquitous winged hourglasses and writhing skeletons became the leitmotif in the *memento mori*, reminders of mortality. Whether ornamenting architecture or stimulating prayer, these decorative devices were intended to prepare the Christian for the inevitability of death, and to promote an interest in the *ars bene moriendi*, the art of dying well.

As Thomas à Kempis suggested in the *Imitation of Christ*, "All your actions, all your thoughts, should be those of one who expects to die before the day is out. Death would have no great terrors for you if you had a quiet conscience."[117]

---

[117] Thomas à Kempis, *The Imitation of Christ* (Milwaukee: Bruce, 1940), 34.

The Death of St. Joseph by Francesco Trevisani

Therefore, the Catholic definition of a good life lay in a good death. To render less fearful the end of bodily life, the arts were constantly called into service. St. Francis of Assisi's poem "The Canticle of the Creatures" encouraged all to praise God "for our sister bodily death, from whom no living man can escape." In striking contrast to what the modern era believes, the era of the Catholic Restoration did not think that the quick death was the best death. The Litany of Saints implores for deliverance from "a sudden and unforeseen death," for as St. Francis said, "Woe on those who die in mortal sin!" Constant vigilance and preparation were needed. Those skeletons that amuse tourists today served as a stern warning: *Hodie mihi, cras tibi* (Today death strikes me, tomorrow you).

In painting, the Catholic Restoration represented the death of St. Joseph as the ideal end for Christian men and women. In Francesco Trevisani's *Death of St. Joseph*, painted for Sant'Ignazio Church in 1712, Jesus' foster father lies on his deathbed while Mary gazes at him devotedly. Jesus stands before him pointing upward authoritatively toward Heaven. Joseph was the first man to know with certainty that he would go to the "house of the Father." St. Joseph illustrates the most peaceful passing in human history. Jesus, radiant, seems to open the heavens so God the Father can welcome him. Soft light gently caresses his moribund face while hosts of angels pray around him.

The revival of the *ars bene moriendi* led to more extravagant representations of death culminating in monuments such as the tomb of Pope Alexander VII in St. Peter's Basilica by Gian Lorenzo Bernini. He built this masterpiece from 1671 to 1678 when he was in his seventies, so death was never far from Bernini's mind. His own preoccupation with a good death inspired Bernini to produce one of his greatest masterpieces. In a breathtaking

Tomb of Pope Alexander VII by Gian Lorenzo Bernini

display of virtuosity, Bernini fashioned a large chunk of red jasper into the form of a theater curtain. Hidden in its billowing folds is a winged bronze skeleton holding up an hourglass. It represents death, always looking to surprise man for "of that day and hour no one knows" (Matt. 24:36). Nonetheless, death does not catch Alexander off guard—the pontiff, bareheaded, with his tiara discarded under his robes, kneels in prayer. The gold and white that surround him indicate that the pope is in a state of grace and is ready to be received into Heaven. Carved out of gleaming Carrara marble, four female figures—Charity, Prudence, Fortitude, and Truth— surround the pope. As a young artist, Bernini loved to amaze audiences with dramatic climaxes—a nymph transformed into a tree, a god abducting a maiden; in his older, wiser years, Bernini captured the greatest moment of transition possible, Alexander's passage from the Church Militant straight to the Church Triumphant.

These ever-present artistic reminders of mortality gave significance and importance to the life of every person, from the most exalted to the humblest. The emphasis on man's every action transformed him into the protagonist of the most important spectacle on earth, his own life. Each decision, reaction, and deed was a choice, like those made by the greatest artists, and the result was the individual work of art, a life to be offered to God when the moment of death came.

Post-Reformation Rome, with its dramatic piazzas opening suddenly off medieval alleyways and its church façades resembling theatrical stages, was created to remind citizens and pilgrims alike that one does not know what waits around the corner and that it behooves the good Christian always to be ready for the curtain to fall. At the same time, the bright marbles, gold accents, and brilliant light effects offered the solace of beauty.

Death is not the end, but the beginning of something more precious than earthly life. The most successful life was ordered to the Last Judgment, when the bodily resurrection would take place and Jesus would return to judge every soul. There would be no more Purgatory; one would be united with Christ in the joy of Heaven or separated for all eternity in the depths of Hell.

THE LAST JUDGMENT

Michelangelo's Last Judgment painting in the Sistine Chapel sparked controversy from the moment of its unveiling on October 31, 1541, during Vespers of All Saints' Day. A contemporary, Nino Sernini, reporting to Cardinal Gonzaga, wrote, "The work is of such beauty that your excellency can imagine that there is no lack of those who condemn it."[118]

For almost five hundred years, the massive fresco has been at the heart of a tug-of-war, some pulling Michelangelo into the Protestant camp (as well as the homosexual, social Darwinist and even the Kabbalah club) while others, ever fewer, have held him firm to the Catholic Faith.

Michelangelo was in his late fifties when he started work on this project, and he had seen a great deal of the Church. He was acutely aware of the Church's need for reform, particularly within the clergy, but he also knew the truth of Church teaching.

This work, inaugurated on the anniversary of Martin Luther's Wittenberg theses, proclaimed Catholic dogma so beautifully that indeed, it could not but cause controversy. In unforgettable imagery, it would assert the responsibilities of the clergy and the

---

[118] Bernadine Ann Barnes, *Michelangelo's Last Judgment: The Renaissance Response*, Discovery Series (Berkeley, CA: University of California Press, 1992), 78.

importance of intercession, exalt the Virgin Mary, and underscore the necessity of cooperation with grace. Every issue raised by the Reformers was given a compelling visual response in Michelangelo's masterpiece.

CLERGY

Michelangelo's ultimate response to the Protestant Reformers started with a rallying cry to the clergy. Placed over the altar wall instead of over the usual entrance and exit, *The Last Judgment* dominated the space intended specifically for clergy, as seen by the rood screen still present in the chapel. The lion's share of the chapel was reserved for the elite, educated members of the papal court who would have plenty of time to study the fresco during the extended liturgies.

The bustle of bodies, the focus on Sts. Peter, Andrew, Bartholomew, and Lawrence—all early Christian priests and deacons who died in bloody witness to Christ—warned the papal court that if Jesus' handpicked followers were crucified, burned, and flayed alive, something similar might be expected from these bishops and cardinals with their benefices and palaces. Unlike in previous versions of this scene, Michelangelo did not label the typical sins of the damned—lust, usury, murder, and gluttony—but indicated only one crime: a figure upside down with keys and a moneybag dangling from his waist: the sale of Church offices. The commerce in relics, indulgences, lucrative Church positions, and especially grace was the most direct route for the clergy to damnation.

Michelangelo included an interesting figure in the lower left corner, however. Tonsured and wearing a religious habit, he is a cleric ministering to the dead—the sixty-year-old artist never downplayed the role played by the clergy in our salvation.

The Last Judgment by Michelangelo Buonarroti

INTERCESSION

Michelangelo produced a jumble of people instead of the neat divisions of earlier images of the Last Judgment. Dismissed as appropriate only "for public baths and taverns" by papal master of ceremonies Biagio da Cesena (thereafter immortalized as donkey-eared Midas in the lower right corner), upon closer inspection the fresco reveals that in the chaos of movement there is a whole lot of saving going on.

On the lower left, angels battle demons to wrest away a single soul, while another man, perhaps St. Dominic, pulls up two people by rosary beads. One man is African and the other Caucasian, illustrating a Church that takes the idea of universal salvation seriously. The missionaries out to convert the people of the new worlds worked ceaselessly to make Heaven as diverse as possible.

Many of the people helping others to rise are not identifiable, perhaps friends, relatives, or souls in Purgatory who received prayers, now coming to assist the newly resurrected. No artist had ever showed such a community in energetic welcome of the saved, nor such a joyous reception into Heaven: people embrace, chatter, and reach out to welcome the crowds of new arrivals.

JESUS

Michelangelo painted Christ like no other in the history of art — his powerful physique and distant expression make Him look unapproachable. The Protestant approach of direct engagement with Jesus seems difficult here. His turned face and raised hand appear to sweep all away before Him. This *"terribile,"* fearsome Christ is a far cry from the gentle sandal-shod shepherd looking for lost sheep or the suffering man on the Cross. He strikes awe into the hapless viewer. The most powerful figure in Michelangelo's formidable repertoire, the musclebound heroic Jesus appears to unleash His full strength, but the fearsome form culminates in His aloof gaze. Painted in profile, Jesus looks strikingly like a stern, distant Grecian statue. How could the faithful find the courage to beg for mercy before such astounding glory?

MARY

Jesus does have one vulnerable area, the wound in His side, left by the spear of Longinus. Here is where Michelangelo chose to paint Mary, Mother of God and the embodiment of the Church. Never before had Mary been depicted intimately nestled by Jesus —she resembles Eve in the center of the Sistine ceiling, emerging from the side of the New Adam.

Michelangelo enshrined Mary as supreme intercessor in the Sistine Chapel. In earlier images, Mary was usually seated below Christ on a lower tier facing John the Baptist, but here Michelangelo placed her next to Jesus. Viewers immediately note the dramatic gesture of the Lord's hand sweeping across His body toward Hell, often missing the gentle fingers curled around the gash in His side beckoning souls to Him. Mary nestles by the wound whence the Church sprang, and she is the conduit to His mercy.

Drawings are the most telling way of understanding an artist's thought process, but Michelangelo, tragically, was notorious for destroying his. But amid the paltry preparatory designs for *The Last Judgment*, two telling ones remain to reveal how the painter arrived at this startling new image.

In the first drawing, the artist placed Mary in her usual seat, slightly lower and to the right of Christ. She leans forward, however, hands clasped in supplication before her Son. The second sketch envisioned Mary approaching Jesus, bowed in deference but with her arms open, as if spreading her mantle of protection, while hopeful souls cluster behind her.

In the final version, Michelangelo boldly settled Mary next to Christ, co-mediatrix and intercessor up to the point of judgment. Mary turns to gaze upon the elect with the same expression used by every painter, from Fra Angelico to Botticelli, in illustrating her response to Gabriel: "Behold, I am the handmaid of the Lord; let it be to me according to your word" (Luke 1:38).

That fiat of Mary, her unwavering yes to God, earned her the highest power of intercession, able to commend souls to her Son on the Last Day. Mary was modeled after a statue of Aphrodite, the Greek goddess of love, and her position next to Christ's body suggests the love of the bridegroom for his bride, the Church. Mary's faithful trust embodies Christ's bride, the Catholic Church, and the most direct means to Heaven.

In recognizing the role of Mary in salvation, the viewer begins to see that the fresco is not as doomsday as it appears — almost everyone in the work is saved, and apparently there are no women in Michelangelo's Hell.

COOPERATION

The most alarming aspect of the work for contemporaries was the proliferation of nude bodies. Not the newly resurrected or the damned — they had always been represented naked as a kind of reminder of their nakedness before God's judgment and the physical suffering experienced in Hell; no, it was the saints and martyrs parading in the heroic nudity of antiquity that shocked less-informed viewers.

The heavenly elect were always clothed — in Giotto's version, in Fra Angelico's, and even in Luca Signorelli's famous chapel in Orvieto. Michelangelo chose not to swathe the saints in draperies, but to give them trophy bodies, those of every athlete who, in the words of St. Paul, "exercises self-control in all things. They do it to receive a perishable wreath, but we an imperishable" (1 Cor. 9:25).

It takes strength and courage to pursue truth. Standing before the revealed truth of Christ is awe-inspiring and fearsome, just as facing the truth about oneself can be painful and discouraging. These saints, probably physically smaller than modern viewers, became larger than life by seeking and bearing witness to truth. There is no room for spiritual pettiness in Michelangelo's Heaven.

Last seen eating locusts in the desert, John the Baptist now looks like Mr. Universe; St. Peter shines as an amazingly well-preserved seventy-year-old; even women such as Catherine of Alexandria show that, in the race to Heaven, the fortitude of the fairer sex equals that of their male counterparts. Each one of the saints used his body, through mortification or mortal sacrifice, for the glory of God. Thus, their resurrected bodies become all the more magnificent for it. These holy heroes and athletes, men and women alike, were meant to be inspirational images to challenge the beholders to greatness.

The first outcry over the painting was over the nudity, disturbing to some of the more hard-core reformers such as Pope Paul IV, who called it "a stew of nudes." Because of the printing press, Michelangelo's bodies eventually became less of a clarion call to glory and more a symbol of an alleged hypocrisy of the Church in wanting to control other people's passions when she couldn't control her own. The Church staved off the destruction of the painting when the Council of Trent ordered the covering of the most "offensive" figures, but today, that powerful voice has lost some of its resonance.

Michelangelo painted *The Last Judgment* just as the seriousness of the Reformation was setting in. What had been intellectual disagreements had escalated into vicious polemics and outright violence. Friends and families were torn apart by faith disputes, made all the more bitterly ironic by the fact that the word *ecclesia* means "people gathered together." The tone of the discourse, whether in printed pamphlets or in public colloquies, grew more strident and divisive; antagonists often selected the harshest words to instigate mobs and to widen the divide among brothers and sisters in Christ.

The post-Reformation populace faced choices and opinions — some informed by personal interpretation of Scripture, others documented by Tradition. In a world in which almost everyone believed in Heaven, Hell, and salvation, these belief decisions were frightening responsibilities, and the tools for making them were at times crude and imprecise. The sheep now had many shepherds, each with his own idea of the perfect pasture.

The terrible responsibility that Christ laid upon the shoulders of St. Peter to "feed my sheep" (John 21:17) had been passed on to the successors of the Prince of the Apostles, and the concern that the sheep might starve in barren pasture weighed heavily. Although the Church had reignited the Inquisition, created an index of banned books, and wielded decrees of excommunication, those harsher methods were generally reserved for persons in danger of leading others astray. For the more rank-and-file faithful, whose beliefs or doubts might never be known in the public arena, the Church had to find a more effective solution for affirming the Faith. One might try to force the sheep back into the pen, as did Calvin's Geneva or Elizabeth's England, but wouldn't it be better if the flock itself wanted to graze in the greener Catholic pasture?[119]

Art provided enticing fodder for the faithful. Pretty and meaningful, it allowed people to stand side by side and face in the same direction instead of in opposition. The skillfully rendered stories appealed to the best in people, while often acknowledging the lost and fallen state of humanity. Art allowed for a more peaceful discourse and easy instruction in the Faith. Art presented saints as familiar friends and sacred stories as actual and applicable, as opposed to dry and dusty.

[119] Rodney Stark, "The Misfortune of State Churches, Forced Piety and Bigotry," in *Reformation Myths: Five Centuries of Misconceptions and (Some) Misfortunes* (London: Society for Promoting Christian Knowledge, 2017), eBook loc. 396–658.

Centuries later, the geniuses who produced these works seem to have been separated from their original mission. The beauty produced by the Catholic Faith to encourage the Catholic Faith seems to have been hijacked: today Caravaggio is seen as an atheist maverick, Artemisia as an angry feminist, Guido Reni as a repressed neurotic, and Bernini, if popular novels are to be believed, as a spokesman for the occult! Their magnificent legacy, forged in one of the most turbulent times for the Faith and in order to reinforce the Faith, has become, at best, a photo-op for bored tourists and, at worst, a vehicle for anti-Catholic propaganda. Catholics, overwhelmed by dubious art history and implacable popular culture, have stepped away from the defense of this art, with the result that it has often become a weapon against doctrine instead of a tool for promoting it.

Looking ahead, perhaps it is time to recover some of the impetus given by these images and the art of this age, to find an engaging way to discuss saints and sacraments in a world grown increasingly accustomed to labels and tirades. Just as the modern entertainment industry offers fifteen minutes of stardom to those desperate for meaning and purpose, the art of the Catholic Restoration could galvanize the faithful and nonfaithful alike to become protagonists on the stage of salvation history, emulating the saints and (bolstered by the sacraments) following Mary, Refuge of Sinners, Loving Mother, and Queen of Heaven, to eternal glory in Christ.

AFTERWORD

———————— ❋ ————————

After visiting the wonders of Catholic art (especially in their original settings in European churches), people often wonder how we can regain our seemingly lost sensitivity to beauty. The Catholic Restoration doesn't owe everything to its prelates; it also owes much to the people who loved their culture, their art, their saints, and their sacred music. Here are a few ideas about how to bring about Catholic Restoration in our own day:

Display Catholic art at home.
Pictures of sunflowers and abstract color combinations may be very *feng shui*, but they won't promote a Catholic culture. I grew up with a copy of Filippo Lippi's *Madonna and Child with Two Angels* in my house, and the first time I saw it in the Uffizi, I felt as if part of me was in that museum. A great many of the wonderful paintings discussed in this book started as private commissions but are in museums today. Familiarity with art breeds love of art, so once you have settled on a work you love, get a copy, and look at it. Admire the delicate painting of a veil, the dramatic glints of light, or a particular color used by the artist. You'll get to know his style, you'll find you like his friends, and

the next thing you know, you'll be delighting friends and family with your knowledge of Catholic art!

Learn the stories of saints.

The saints led amazing lives, touched by grace. Some are swash-buckling, some are funny (read Catherine of Siena telling the Lord what's what, or St. Jerome mocking the Roman gods), some overcome huge personal problems, some are special from birth. The more you know their stories, the more you own them; and soon you'll not only instantly recognize the star of the painting, but you'll be able to share these stories with others. The life and times of Joan of Arc are more interesting and exciting than those of the stars of reality shows, yet it is the ins and outs of today's icons of popular culture that people can recite, not the life of a Camillus de Lellis who went from being semi-crippled gambler to the inventor of the field ambulance.

Furthermore, these great saints had Annibale, Lavinia, and Michelangelo as their cinematographers and stylists, not some name-less Hollywood troupe. I grew up reading biographies and stories of great figures from the past, and it was seeing the happy union of words and images that made me decide to study art history.

Visit Catholic art in museums.

Sometimes we walk through the shoe department of a favorite store or stop by a beloved restaurant for just a glass of wine. So, too, museums can be part of the regular fabric of life. A museum visit (short of the Louvre or the Vatican Museums) doesn't need to be a big production; just a short stroll through a few galler-ies, stopping and looking at whatever catches your eye, can be delightful and refreshing. Bring kids and ask them to describe shapes, scenes, and colors to expand their visual sensitivity and vocabulary, both sorely needed to maintain a civilized discourse. Let them tell the stories of the works and figure out who is who in the picture — this is how one learns to read art, recognize attributes, and claim one's Catholic cultural inheritance.

Encourage Catholic art.
If you are in a position to buy paintings, learn to be a good patron. If you see someone good at landscapes, suggest a Garden of Eden, Agar in the Desert, Francis Receiving the Stigmata, or Margaret of Cortona finding her lifeless lover. The great painters of the Catholic Restoration became great because they had many interested and demanding patrons. As writers gravitate to New York or Hollywood, artists gravitate to places where there is work and where there are the types of challenges that can make them famous.

Develop Catholic pride
Don't shy away from Michelangelo because of his rumored homosexuality. His art is not about sex; it is about salvation. Take back the great story unfolding on the canvases, instead of watching them be hijacked. Caravaggio killed a man in a fit of anger, a crime that indirectly cost him his life, but his struggle with prideful rage produced compelling lessons on the humility of saints. In recent years, Artemisia may have been co-opted by man-hating, abortion-loving feminism, but she is not lost. Reclaim her messy paintings of Judith as images of a woman conquering evil, painted by a woman who herself wrestled with sin. None of our painters has been canonized, and only one has been declared blessed: Fra Angelico. Although plenty of these artists are in Heaven, when you follow them, look to the path they painted rather than the path they took.

LIVES OF THE ARTISTS

———— ✢ ————

Ever since Giorgio Vasari first published his *Lives of the Artists* in 1550, stories of the training, achievements, and personal quirks of the most famous painters, sculptors, and architects have been a mainstay of the history of art. The array of names involved with the art of the Catholic Restoration can be overwhelming and easy to mix up, so it is my hope that these miniature biographies might entice you to get to know more about these artists and that they will one day surprise you as old friends as you walk through museums and galleries worldwide. There are thirty-two biographies, organized in order of dates so that you can see how influences and ideas developed from one generation to the next.

MICHELANGELO BUONARROTI (1475–1564)

Michelangelo was born in Florence just as the Renaissance was reaching its zenith. A painter, sculptor, and architect, he would carve the *David* and paint the Sistine Chapel in his thirties, defining a new standard for Renaissance art. He outlived both Raphael and Leonardo and navigated the turbulent changes of the Reformation era. Although modern art history prefers to view him as sympathetic to the Protestant cause and beliefs,

Michelangelo was a third-order Franciscan who remained faithful to the Catholic Church and supportive of both Pope Paul III, who called the Council of Trent, and the new religious orders that cropped up in his old age, the Oratorians and the Jesuits. He died while building the basilica of St. Peter (free of charge) at the age of eighty-nine.

ANDREA DEL SARTO (1486–1530)

Although he died before the Reformation got into full swing, Florentine Andrea del Sarto witnessed the first dark clouds of heresy to darken the Renaissance sky. He was trained under Piero di Cosimo, an eccentric but technically brilliant painter, and his style was forged when he came to Rome in 1510 and saw the frescoes by Raphael under way in the Vatican. Called "unambitious" by his student and later biographer Giorgio Vasari, Andrea nonetheless innovated the iconography of the Sacred Conversation and the Pietà during his short life. He was invited to France by Francis I to join another Florentine genius, Leonardo da Vinci. He stayed only briefly, however, apparently because of his wife's jealousy. Andrea died of the plague in Florence at the age of forty-three.

TITIAN (1488–1576)

The long career of Titian Vecellio of Cadore spanned the heights of the Renaissance to the Catholic Restoration after the Council of Trent. As a young student in Venice, he made his name using soft, blended colors that lent themselves both to captivating altarpieces as well as to seductive erotic art. For many years he produced such works for the Holy Roman Emperor Charles V and later for King Philip II of Spain. Personal tragedy and the spiritually charged atmosphere of the Reformation stimulated Titian to produce some of the finest religious painting of the age.

He was brought to Rome by Pope Paul III and even attended one of the sessions of the Council of Trent. Later in life, his works were darker, with asymmetrical compositions and the use of rays of light to illuminate the action. This powerful painting reflected the turbulent age, becoming at times almost an impressionistic vision of saints, sacraments, and salvation in the flux of the Reformation.

POMARANCIO (1517–1596)

Born Niccolò Circignani in Pomarancio, this distinctive painter shares this nickname with two other artists. Pomarancio was among the first out of the starting gate for painting in the Catholic Restoration, coming to Rome to paint the Vatican palace alongside Santi di Tito and Barocci just at the moment when the Council of Trent was drawing to a close. In 1579 he returned to Rome, this time to paint for Pope Gregory XIII with Mattheus Brill, a Flemish landscape artist. This collaboration would lead to Pomarancio's relationship with the Jesuits and his famous martyrdom cycle in Santo Stefano Rotondo. Pomarancio would spend several years between painting in Rome's oldest churches, such as Sts. Giovanni and Paolo, as well as the newest, such as the Gesù. He produced a fresco cycle for the Church of the Holy Cross, one of Rome's most venerated sites of pilgrimage. As of the late 1590s, his graphic style fell out of fashion, which prompted Pomarancio to move out toward the more provincial town of Perugia, where he died.

BARTOLOMEO PASSAROTTI (1529–1592)

"Passarotto" in Italian means "little sparrow" and this fascinating although eccentric painter often signed his works by depicting this bird. Bartolomeo went to Rome in the 1550s and worked there alongside the Zuccari brothers. He maintained ties with the Eternal City, especially during the reign of Pope Gregory XIII, who, like Passarotti, was Bolognese. Passarotti's success in painting began just as Gabriele Paleotti arrived in Bologna to be installed as the new archbishop. Bartolomeo's friendships spanned scientists and prelates: Ignazio Danti spoke fondly of him and Ulisse Aldrovandi, a professor at the University of Bologna called "the father of natural history," often consulted with him. Unconventional and engaging, Passarotti pioneered the genre style, producing striking images of anything from butchers in their shop to drawings of hybrid fauna to portraits of botany professors. He greatly influenced the Carracci as they began their careers in a city dominated by Passarotti's striking artistic personality.

FEDERICO BAROCCI (1535–1612)

Born Federico Fiori in Urbino, the hometown of Raphael, Barocci came to Rome for the first time in the 1550s as a student. There he met the aging master Michelangelo, who encouraged him in his work. He returned to Rome a decade later, working on frescoes in the Vatican Belvedere Palace for Pope Pius IV, but he fell ill and, thinking himself poisoned by a jealous rival, returned to Urbino. Despite his distance from the patronage capital of Rome and his refusal to return, Barocci's reputation was such that the Oratorians, the Holy Roman Emperor Rudolph II, King Philip II of Spain, and Pope Clement VIII all vied for his works. He was meticulous in preparing his work: more than two thousand drawings by his hand exist, more than any other artist. Barocci produced almost exclusively religious paintings and was a lay member of the newly formed Capuchin order, which, after a rocky start, was one of the most effective congregations of the Catholic Restoration. His funeral was attended by people and dignitaries from far and wide, and he was buried in the Church of St. Francis in Urbino.

FEDERICO ZUCCARI (1540–1609)

Federico came to Rome at the age of eleven to assist his brother Taddeo and thrived in the artistic environment of the Eternal City. At twenty-one, he was frescoing the Casino Pio IV, the philosopher's garden of St. Charles Borromeo, and four years later he was inducted into the prestigious Roman Painting Academy. He worked on the cathedrals of Florence and Orvieto; Cardinal Alessandro Farnese employed him for several projects; and he spent three years as the court painter of Philip II of Spain. Zuccari had a reputation as a troublemaker, as swift to use his drawing skill for a savage satire as for a sacred scene. He disdained the art of Caravaggio, dismissing him out of hand: "What is all the fuss about? I see nothing more than the style of Giorgione." This peripatetic painter traveled from England to Brussels to Venice yet managed to write a historiography of painters before he died in 1609 in Ancona.

DOMENICO FONTANA (1543–1607)

From Canton Ticino on Lake Lugano in Switzerland, Domenico moved to Rome as Michelangelo's years as head architect of St. Peter's were drawing to a close. He began working as a stucco artist but soon became architect to Cardinal Felice Peretti, who was planning a new chapel for his tomb in St. Mary Major. When Cardinal Peretti was elected Pope Sixtus V in 1585, Domenico's fortunes rose as well. He was nominated head architect of St. Peter's in 1585 and appointed to work on St. John Lateran the following year. He designed roads, fountains, and churches, and his organizational skills were legendary, but his feat in moving the 327-ton obelisk from the side of St. Peter's to the front, intact, recorded in his own account of the work, earned him a special place in the history of the basilica. Upon the death of Sixtus, the jealousies and accusations rife among the denizens of the papal court saw Domenico dismissed from his position. The viceroy of Naples seized the opportunity to hire Domenico, and after constructing the royal palace and several other buildings, he died, leaving a legacy of urban planning that would lead Europe into the modern era.

FRANCESCO BASSANO (1549–1592)

Born in the Italian region of Veneto, Francesco was the eldest son of the famous Jacopo, a prolific painter who pioneered land-scape, genre, and night-scene paintings. Raised in turbulent Ven-ice in the wake of the Reformation, Francesco and his father worked side by side on major religious commissions throughout the region. The Bassanos' fame extended to Rome, where, in the last decade of the sixteenth century, the construction of new churches required numerous new altarpieces. Bassano worked for the Gesù and St. Louis of the French in Rome and perhaps would have gone on to glory in the Eternal City, but he suffered from what contemporaries called "an excess of melancholy" and, in a fit of paranoia, jumped out of a window. Francesco died from his injuries in 1592, a few months after the death of his father.

LAVINIA FONTANA (1552–1614)

The daughter of successful Mannerist painter Prospero Fontana, Lavinia grew up in a privileged and cultured circle in Bologna. A reversal in her father's economic fortunes, however, meant that Lavinia would need to forge a career for herself through painting. Starting with portraits of Bolognese noblewomen, she became the first female professional painter, largely supported by Gabriele Paleotti. The archbishop of Bologna helped her to secure her the first commission for an altarpiece to be done by a woman in both Bologna and Rome. Lavinia was married to Paolo Zappi, with whom she had eleven children and who supported her career in every possible way. She was the first woman inducted into painting in Rome, and she died after a successful and respected career in the Eternal City. She is buried in Santa Maria sopra Minerva.

LUDOVICO CARRACCI (1555–1619)

The cousin of Agostino and Annibale, Ludovico was one of the driving minds of the Carracci painting academy. He studied under Prospero Fontana, the father of Lavinia. Perhaps in that studio, which collaborated so closely with Archbishop Paleotti, Ludovico developed a particular interest in religious art, searching for ways to engage viewers with greater intensity. While most painters looked to Rome for guidance, Ludovico was interested in the Leonardo da Vinci–like sfumato of Parma and Venice. His fervor for religious art brought him commissions for frescoes, altarpieces, and devotional works throughout the Italian peninsula. His images of visionary experiences effectively used soft color and looser brushstroke to draw the viewer into an almost dreamlike world of mysticism. His former student, Guido Reni, would become Ludovico's bitterest rival, with his crisp colors and restrained scenes almost rebuking the exuberant art of Ludovico.

AGOSTINO CARRACCI (1557–1602)

In many ways the brains of the Carracci school, Agostino was best suited to run the public relations machine for the family. Older than his exceptionally talented brother Annibale, he circulated among patrons and elites, explaining the academy's artistic theories. "Real painters talk with their hands," Annibale once rebuked Agostino, but Agostino's skill in engraving and his versatility in pleasing potential patrons helped propel the success of the school. He was a very gifted teacher, able to transmit ideas and techniques to students such as Lanfranco and Domenichino. Although never achieving the artistic fame of his brother or cousin, Agostino produced many lovely altarpieces for churches throughout Italy.

DOMENICO PASSIGNANO (1559–1638)

Born to the Cresti family in the hamlet of Passignano a few miles south of Florence, Domenico traded small-town life for the great urban centers, going in 1575 to Florence, where he worked under Federico Zuccari on the frescoes in the Duomo of Florence. He went to Rome with his master, where he produced works for Chiesa Nuova and the Farnese family and earned the favor of Clement VIII, who knighted him. Despite his central Italian roots, Domenico's style was steeped in Venetian influence, especially the tenebrism and striking diagonal compositions of Tintoretto. Returning to Florence, he worked for the Grand Duke Ferdinand and his wife, Christina of Lorraine, producing many works for the Medici, including a celebrated portrait of Galileo.

ANNIBALE CARRACCI (1560–1609)

In an Italy made up of separate and rival city-states, Annibale artistically united the peninsula with his appreciation of all the painting styles of Italy. Incorporating the best of Venetian color, Florentine line, Emilian naturalism, and Roman grandeur, Annibale developed an eclectic style coveted by every European court. Together with his brother Agostino and his cousin Ludovico, he founded an art academy in his native Bologna. His school would ultimately produce some of the finest Counter-Reformation artists—Reni, Guercino, and Domenichino, among others. The school focused on drawing from life, as opposed to ancient sculpture, and infused a fresh immediacy into religious painting. Annibale was a favorite of the Farnese family and executed many works for them, before a mysterious "melancholy" overtook him, rendering him unable to paint for the last four years of his life. Annibale died in Rome and was buried in the Pantheon, at his request, next to his hero, Raphael.

VENTURA SALIMBENI (1568–1613)

A native of Siena, Ventura spent most of his life working in Tuscany and Umbria on major fresco commissions. His style was formed in Rome, however, where he went at age twenty to work on one of the many decorative projects of Pope Sixtus V, but he was soon commissioned to work in both the Gesù and St. Mary Major. During his time in Rome he was influenced by the art of Barocci and Cavaliere D'Arpino. His style, formed in the first exciting years of Catholic Restoration, served him well, and he achieved great success painting images exalting doctrine and the sacraments with his careful clarity and his delightful colors. Like Agostino Carracci, he was an expert printmaker, using his etchings to diffuse images of his work. This contributed to his very successful career even outside the main patronage center of Rome.

CAVALIERE D'ARPINO (1568–1640)

Although Arpino was his family's town of origin, Giuseppe Cesari was born in Rome. He earned the title "Cavaliere" when he was made a Knight of Christ by his patron Clement VIII. Like

Gaspare Celio, Giuseppe studied under Niccolò Circignani, although he would become much more successful, especially for large-scale commissions. His star rose under Pope Clement in preparation for the Jubilee Year of 1600, when he was overloaded with commissions. He began work on the ceiling in the Contarelli Chapel in San Luigi dei Francesi but abandoned it in 1593. Caravaggio, for a while a studio hand in the busy workshop of Cesari, would rise to stardom completing the commission in 1600. From designing mosaics for St. Peter's to decorating the great villas of Frascati, Cesari was one of the most in-demand artists of his age. He was helpful to younger artists, most notably Guido Reni, and universally hailed as one of Rome's greatest painters. Upon his death in 1640, he was accorded the honor of burial in St. John Lateran, the cathedral of Rome.

GASPARE CELIO (1571–1640)

Born and raised in Rome, Gaspare left the city only once to work for the Farnese family in Parma. He studied under Niccolò Circignani (Pomarancio), a favorite of the Jesuits and the artist of the Santo Stefano martyrdom cycle. Gaspare, in his turn, was chosen at age twenty-four by the Society of Jesus to work with Fr. Giuseppe Valeriano on the Passion Chapel of the Gesù. He went on to work in Santa Maria sopra Minerva, but his feud with Giovanni Baglione damaged his reputation, and works were scarce after that. Gaspare wrote what is considered to be the first art historical guidebook to Rome, *Memoria delli nomi dell'artefici delle pitture che sono in alcune chiese, facciate e palazzi di Roma*, describing the contemporary art scene in Rome in the first half of the seventeenth century. Unfortunately, his dislike of Caravaggio and Baglione ensured that there would be no mention of their works, and thus Gaspare's book slipped into oblivion.

CARAVAGGIO (1571–1610)

Born Michelangelo Merisi in the Milan of Charles Borromeo, Caravaggio went to Rome in the 1590s trained in oil and more prepared for still-life painting than for historical fresco cycles. Earning the protection of Cardinal del Monte, a friend of the Medici princes, Caravaggio saw doors open for him as of 1600, when he became one of the major painters of the Jubilee Year. Hired by the most coveted patrons of the age, Caravaggio proved himself able to translate the ideas of the post-Tridentine Church into powerful, attention-getting art. Unreliable both personally and professionally (several of his works were rejected out of hand), Caravaggio is known primarily through prison records and old enemies settling scores. His glittering career in Rome was cut short when he murdered a man in 1606, and despite successful commissions in Naples, Malta, and Sicily, his goal was a papal pardon to return to Rome. He died of malaria in 1610, one hundred miles north of Rome.

GUIDO RENI (1575–1642)

Divine Guido, as he was called in his day, hailed from Bologna, the second city in importance in the Papal States after Rome. After studying in the Mannerist studio of Denis Calvaert, he joined the Carracci academy, where he spent another nine years. The grace he learned from Calvaert and the naturalism he drew from the Carracci combined to create one of the most recognizable styles of the Catholic Restoration. Employed in Rome by the Borghese to paint everything from the new papal palace on the Quirinal to the pleasure villas of Scipione, the cardinal's nephew, Guido's star rose swiftly in Rome. An altercation with the ambassador of the king of Spain sent Guido back to his native city, where he ran one of the biggest studios with the highest output of the age. His style, restrained, elegant, and graceful, was considered by many churchmen to be the ideal form of Catholic Restoration art.

STEFANO MADERNO (1576–1636)

Stefano's origins are debated, but it seems that he may have been related to Carlo Maderno, who served as head architect of St. Peter's until his death in 1629. Trained by a Flemish sculptor in Rome, Stefano showed tremendous potential to become sculpture's great innovator until he was overshadowed by the rise of Bernini. The late sixteenth century had not been kind to sculpture, producing awkwardly posed, hipshot figures with elongated limbs that were neither inspiring or engaging. The clean lines of Maderno swept in like a breath of fresh air. Only twenty-three when he carved the hauntingly lovely Santa Cecilia after the rediscovery of her body, Stefano went on to produce a statue of Charles Borromeo right after his canonization and a figure of St. Peter for the new papal residence in the Quirinal Palace. His talents were undermined when he was granted an important position in the office of excises, and his duties left little time for art. He was later invited to work at the Holy House of Loreto, but his style was no longer appreciated in the dramatic era of the Baroque.

PETER PAUL RUBENS (1577–1640)

This flamboyant Fleming was fundamentally formed in Rome as an artist. Converting to Catholicism at eleven, when he moved to Antwerp with his mother, he trained there, studying Italian engravings. In 1600, the year of the great Jubilee of Clement VIII, Rubens went to Italy, visiting Venice, Florence, Rome, and Genoa before settling for a few years in Mantua as court painter to the Gonzaga family. In Rome, he was taken by the power of Caravaggio's art and was instrumental in getting the painter known in northern Italy and later in Europe. Returning to Antwerp, he set up shop, always planning to go back to Italy, but it would never happen. Instead, Rubens brought Italy to Belgium: the monumental sizes of his works, the powerful brush-strokes lending vivacity to his stories, and the dizzying color proclaimed the Catholic Faith with pride and joy. A deeply faith-ful man committed to his Church, Rubens enjoyed the trust of the Hapsburg rulers and worked as a diplomatic envoy between England and Spain. He died leaving eight children, one of the most successful, happy, and devout painters in the history of art.

CARLO SARACENI (1579–1620)

The short life of Carlo Saraceni contrasts sharply with his vast artistic production and his swift stylistic development. Born in Venice, Saraceni was originally influenced by the number of Flemish artists arriving at the end of the century in the Serene Republic, particularly by Adam Elsheimer. At first, Carlo special-ized in small paintings on copper and landscapes, but he moved to Rome in 1600 just as Caravaggio's Contarelli Chapel was coming into completion. He took well to religious painting, employing elements of Caravaggio's tenebrism with his own splendid flour-ishes of light and color. When both Elsheimer and Caravaggio died in 1610, their patrons turned to Saraceni. A Francophile, he spoke French, dressed in French fashions, and taught several of the budding French artists in the city.

DOMENICHINO (1581–1641)

Bolognese Domenico Zampieri was called by the diminutive, "Do-menichino" for his short stature. One of the finest students of the Carracci academy, he was initially taunted as "the ox" because he worked so slowly and was taciturn, but Annibale Carracci responded that "the ox" plowed the most fertile soil and would one day nourish painting. He came to Rome assisted by Cardinale Girolamo Agucchi, who was working on a treatise on painting. Domenichino became one of the great promoters of the classical Baroque, dramatic but with pure lines and crisp images. He drew envy everywhere he went, and in Rome a fellow student from the Carracci academy accused him of plagiarism. Nonetheless, Domenichino was in constant demand in Rome and elsewhere, working for Cardinal Aldobrandini, the Theatines, the Oratorians, and Rome's elite, and was eventually invited to Naples to work for the viceroy. Here Domenichino experienced such rivalry and envy from the local artists that he grew increasingly fearful for his life. He died in Naples at age sixty, and his unfinished commissions were parceled out to his rivals.

DOMENICO FETTI (1589–1623)

Domenico was a rarity in the Catholic Restoration: a Roman painter who left the world of copious and lucrative art commissions to seek his fortune in Northern Italy. Educated with the Jesuits at the Collegio Romano, he left in 1613 to become the painter to the court of Mantua. From 1618 to 1622, he painted a series of New Testament parables in landscape or genres settings, fruit of his study of both Caravaggio and Elsheimer. These works were startling in their lovely simplicity and therefore earned him the enmity of the local artists. Fetti was very taken with the art of Peter Paul Rubens, who had spent some time at the Mantuan court, and began to change his palette for more dazzling colors, like those of the Belgian master. In 1623, Fetti decided to move to Venice, but died the following year, before his next great stage of artistic development could flower.

Guercino (1591–1666)

Francesco Barbieri, born in Cento, near Bologna, was given the nickname Guercino for an eye defect from infancy. This defect, however, did not impede him from becoming one of the most successful and prolific painters of the Carracci school. His early work reflected the style of Ludovico, with crowded compositions and rapid brushstrokes conveying movement. He found an admirer in Pope Gregory XV, who brought him to Rome and gave him many commissions, culminating in the twenty-three-foot altarpiece of *The Death of St. Petronilla* for St. Peter's Basilica. Guercino eventually moved back to Bologna and took over the studio of Guido Reni after the latter's death in 1642. At this point, he changed his style for a more restrained look, allowing more space in his compositions and tightening his brushstroke. Through both stages of his career, however, he employed a stunning blue pigment, a jeweled tone similar to lapis, which remained like a signature in all his work. A deeply religious man, Guercino died in Forli on Christmas Eve, 1666.

Artemisia Gentileschi (1593–1656)

Daughter of Caravaggio crony Orazio Gentileschi, Artemisia grew up surrounded by the stimulating but risky Roman art scene. Her father trained her alongside her brothers, and her skills, particularly in drawing the female body, outshone those of everyone in her family. Sheltered by her father, given his rough crowd of associates, she was nonetheless raped at age seventeen by one of his collaborators, Agostino Tassi. After a painful rape trial, she was hastily married to an inferior painter and moved to Florence. There she flourished, feted by the Medici court, and, on the recommendation of Galileo, was inducted as the first woman of the Florentine Academy of Design. A restless figure, Artemisia never settled down, returning to Rome, then traveling to Naples, taking commissions in London, and then moving back to Naples, where she died, perhaps of the plague, at sixty-three.

NICCOLÒ TORNIOLI (1598–1651)

Sienese painter Niccolò Tornioli owed his success to a series of cardinals with excellent taste. He started in the retinue of Milanese Federico IV Borromeo but was soon noticed by Francesco Barberini, nephew of Pope Urban VIII. It was when Tornioli offered to paint stories from the life of St. Philip free of charge for the Oratorians in Chiesa Nuova that the Spada family recognized the genius of the artist. Cardinal Virgilio Spada took him as the family artist, collecting seven of his works. Using the tenebrism of Caravaggio but the organized compositions of the Carracci, Tornioli's works were pleasing for their dramatic intensity as well as the sumptuous fabrics depicted. After a falling out with the Spada cardinal while working in the Blessed Sacrament Chapel in St. Peter's Basilica, Tornioli's professional reputation was destroyed, and he died shortly thereafter.

GIAN LORENZO BERNINI (1598–1680)

The undisputed superstar of Rome's Baroque age, Gian Lorenzo Bernini was the son of the court sculptor to Pope Paul V and was "discovered" working with his father in Santa Maria Maggiore at age fifteen. He trained among the greatest works of art in the Vatican and was formed in the Rome of Galileo and St. Robert Bellarmine. Bernini went on to become head architect of St. Peter's in his twenties, and, together with a succession of popes, he reshaped the Eternal City with fountains and piazzas, transforming it into an extensive stage set. Bernini loved theater, both producing and directing plays, but he also loved his Faith, as attested by Fr. Giovanni Paolo Oliva, who said that conversing with Bernini was like talking to a graduate student in theology. His son, a priest, records that his father prepared carefully for the end of life, dying what the seventeenth century would define as a textbook good death, and was humbly buried in St. Mary Major, his favorite church.

CARLO CIGNANI (1628–1719)

Like many of art's greatest innovators in this period, Carlo Cignani was born in Bologna, the second city of the papal states after Rome. A descendant of the Carracci school, he studied under Francesco Albani, one of the first pupils of Annibale. He spent only a short stint in Rome, choosing to forge most of his career in Emilia-Romagna. His pleasant and unassuming personality led him to live simply, so much so that he has been overlooked in the annals of art history in favor of his more flamboyant peers. His style, elegant, polished, and intellectual, enlivened by strong color contrasts, was transmitted through his school, which emphasized drawing from life. Generous with his knowledge, Carlo left many pupils, including Giuseppe Maria Crespi.

GIOVANNI BATTISTA GAULLI (1639–1709)

Giovanni Battista Gaulli hailed from Genoa and was known by his nickname, Baccicia (a local abbreviation for Giovanni Battista). While in his twenties, he moved to Rome, where he found success as a painter of altarpieces. A trip to Parma at the age of thirty awakened an interest in sweeping dramatic vault frescoes, and his style changed to a looser, more energetic painting technique. A protégé of Gian Lorenzo Bernini, he was chosen at age twenty-two to become the official painter of the Gesù Church in Rome. His dynamic decoration of the vast spaces of the Gesù cupola, apse, and vault gave rise to the description of his art as Bernini in paint. His influence can be felt in many of the most celebrated ceiling frescoes in Rome.

GIOVANNI BATTISTA CRESPI (1573–1632)

Giovanni Battista Crespi was also called "Il Cerano" for the little village outside Milan where he made his home. Gifted at painting and sculpture as well as architecture, he dedicated his numerous talents to producing art in keeping with the spirit of the Catholic Restoration. In his twenties, Crespi spent some time in Rome, where he was influenced by the art and color of Barocci. Returning to Milan, Crespi painted a series of large canvases of the life of St. Charles Borromeo for the cathedral, which are still displayed on the saint's feast day. Crespi excelled at mystical paintings, simplifying and humanizing scenes of ecstasies and visions. In 1620, Cardinal Federico Borromeo, cousin of St. Charles, invited the scholarly artist to lead his Academy of St. Ambrose and appointed him director of decoration for the cathedral, which Crespi remained until his death at age fifty-nine.

MARCO BENEFIAL (1684–1764)

Marco Benefial belongs to the swan song of Catholic art. Raised in Rome, he studied with Carlo Cignani, an artistic lineage that traces directly back to the Carracci school. His first work, *The Apotheosis of St. Philip Neri*, was rejected, and Benefial responded by hanging it in a pharmacist's shop near the Pantheon, his home neighborhood. Frustrated by the mediocrity of early eighteenth-century religious painting, he fought to change the rules for teaching drawing, hoping to bring art back to its glorious days of Carracci naturalism and more controlled composition. He drew Pope Clement IX to his side but alienated many of his peers.

Although a very successful portrait artist because of his naturalistic tendency, he was first and foremost a splendid draftsman, and some of his finest works still hang unnoticed in Roman churches, such as *The Stories of Margaret of Cortona* in the Church of Aracoeli, painted for her canonization in 1728.

ACKNOWLEDGMENTS

———————— ❊ ————————

As the five hundredth anniversary of the Protestant Reformation loomed, I proposed a series of articles to Elizabeth Scalia, then English editor of Aleteia news service. She immediately supported the idea and encouraged me throughout the year in the "When Art Came to the Rescue" series, which would become this book. Charlie McKinney of Sophia Institute Press then providentially appeared and suggested transforming the often-random articles into a book, and my editor, John Barger, has patiently polished it into this finished product.

This book started far earlier than the above thanks would suggest, however. It owes its DNA to my professors at the University of Bologna who encouraged me to do my graduate work on the Bolognese painters of the Counter-Reformation and planted the seeds not only of this book but of my return to the Faith through this same art. My cradle-Catholic friends Gregory DiPippo, Fr. Michael Keating, and the late Don Briel were invaluable in the long process of identifying the issues of the age that the art addressed, and my Catholic-convert friends Steve and Janet Ray helped me to understand the Protestant arguments and how the artwork responded to them.

I owe my students at Duquesne University and Christendom College many thanks for studying these topics as the ideas took shape in the form of a course, and for asking the right questions that opened my eyes to new insights. The Vatican Museums allowed me to write and lecture on this topic for our in-house guide-formation classes; the encouragement of their direction and staff has made this book possible.

But without my family, this project would never have made it off the ground. The patience of my children, Claire, Giulia, and Joshua, during those long silent hours of writing, and the precious advice of my mother, Mary Ann Glendon, were instrumental to this book. The greatest thanks, however, go to my husband, Thomas Williams, who read every line, discussed every theme, made tactful suggestions and corrections, and kept me on course.

A final thanks to Michelangelo, Caravaggio, Lavinia Fontana, and Annibale Carracci for their witness in paint and marble, so powerful and persuasive that it served as a beacon to guide me back to the Catholic fold.

PHOTO CREDITS

Photo Credits

Photo Credits

BIBLIOGRAPHY

Albertini, Francesco. *Trattato Dell'angelo Custode*. Rome: Bartolommeo Zannetti, 1612.

Alighieri, Dante. *Divine Comedy*. Translated by Allen Mandelbaum. Berkeley: University of California Press, 1980.

Ambrose. "Sermon 22, Section 30." http://www.documentacatholicaomnia.eu/02m/0339-0397,_Ambrosius,_In Psalmum_David_CXVIII_Expositio,_MLT.pdf.

Aquinas, St. Thomas. *Summa Theologica*. New Advent, http://www.newadvent.org/summa/.

Argan, Giulio Carlo, and Bruno Contardi. *Michelangelo Architect*. London: Thames and Hudson, 1993.

Bacci, Pietro Giacomo. *The Life of Saint Philip Neri: Apostle of Rome and Founder of the Congregation of the Oratory*. 2nd ed. London: Paternoster House, 1902.

Bailey, Gauvin A. *Between Renaissance and Baroque: Jesuit Art in Rome, 1565–1610*. Toronto: University of Toronto Press, 1999.

Baker, William. *A Plain Exposition of the Thirty-Nine Articles of the Church of England*. London: Francis and John Rivington, 1883.

Barnes, Bernadine Ann. *Michelangelo's Last Judgment: The Renaissance Response*. Discovery Series. Berkeley, CA: University of California Press, 1992.

Bäumer, Remigius. "Reformation." In *Marienlexikon*. St. Ottilien: EOS Verlag, 1992.

Bellori, Giovanni Pietro, Alice Sedgwick Wohl, Hellmut Wohl, and Tomaso Montanari. *The Lives of the Modern Painters, Sculptors and Architects*. New York: Cambridge University Press, 2005.

Benedict XVI, Pope. Address to Clergy of Bolzano-Bressanone, August 6, 2008. https://w2.vatican.va/content/benedict-xvi/en/speeches/2008/august/documents/hf_ben-xvi_spe_20080806_clero-bressanone.html.

———. *Introduction to Christianity*. San Francisco: Ignatius Press, 1990.

Bernard of Clairvaux. *St. Bernard's Sermons on the Canticle of Canticles*. Dublin: Browne and Nolan, 1920.

Borromeo, Federico. *Sacred Painting: Museum*. Edited and translated by Kenneth Sprague Rothwell. Tatti Renaissance Library. Cambridge, MA: Harvard University Press, 2010.

Borromeo, Charles. *Charles Borromeo: Selected Orations, Homilies and Writings*. Edited by John R. Cihak. Translated by Ansgar Santogrossi. London: Bloomsbury, 2017.

Brown, Dan. *Angels and Demons*. New York: Pocket Books, 2006.

Calvin, John, and Henry Beveridge. *Institutes of the Christian Religion*. Grand Rapids, MI: Wm. B. Eerdmans, 1989.

Calvin, John. *Commentaries on St. Paul's Epistles to Timothy, Titus and Philemon*. Altenmünster, Germany: Jazzybee Verlag, 2012.

———. "Letter to Charles V on the Necessity of Reforming the Church" (1543). Protestant Heritage Press, http://www.swrb.com/newslett/actualNLs/NRC_ch02.htm.

Caravale, Giorgio. *Preaching and Inquisition in Renaissance Italy: Words on Trial*. Translated by Frank Gordon. Catholic Christendom, 1300–1700. Leiden: Brill, 2016.

Catholic University of America. *New Catholic Encyclopedia*. 2nd ed. 15 vols. Detroit: Thomson/Gale, 2003.

Chillingworth, William. *The Religion of Protestants: A Safe Way to Salvation*. London: Henry Bohn, 1846.

Christiansen, Keith. "Barocci, the Franciscans and a Possible Funerary Gift." *Burlington Magazine* 147 (2005): 722–728.

Chrysostom, John. Harkins. *Baptismal Instructions*. Translated by Paul W. Harkins. Ancient Christian Writers. Westminster, MD: Newman Press, 1963.

Cole, William. "Was Luther a Devotee of Mary?" *Marian Studies* 21 (1970).

Gerson, Jean, and André Combes. *De Mystica Theologia*. Theasaurus Mundi Bibliotheca Scriptorum Latinorum Mediae et Recentioris Aetatis. Rome: In Aedibus Theasure Mundi, 1968.

Goodier, Alban. *Saints for Sinners*. New York: Image Books, 1959.

Gregory the Great. *Forty Gospel Homilies*. Translated by David Hurst. Cistercian Studies Series. Kalamazoo, MI: Cistercian Publications, 1990.

Gregory the Great. *The Dialogues of Saint Gregory, Surnamed the Great; Pope of Rome and the First of That Name. Divided into Four Books, Wherein He Entreateth of the Lives and Miracles of the Saints in Italy and of the Eternity of Men's Souls*. Edited by Edmund G. Gardner. London: P. L. Warner, 1906.

Hall, Marcia B. *After Raphael: Painting in Central Italy in the Sixteenth Century*. Cambridge: Cambridge University Press, 1999.

Hardon, John A. *The History of Eucharistic Adoration: Development of Doctrine in the Catholic Church*. Oak Lawn, IL: CMJ Marian Publishers, 1991.

Harris, Enriqueta. *Complete Studies on Velázquez*. Madrid: Centro de Estudios Europa Hispánica, 2006.

Hibbard, Howard. *Caravaggio*. Icon Editions. New York: Harper and Row, 1983.

Hoffer, Eric. *The True Believer: Thoughts on the Nature of Mass Movements*. New York: Harper and Row, 1951.

Ignatius of Loyola. *The Spiritual Exercises of St. Ignatius of Loyola*. Translated by Elder Mullan, S.J. New York: P. J. Kennedy and Sons, 1914.

Ignatius of Loyola, St. *Personal Writings: Reminiscences, Spiritual Diary, Select Letters Including the Text of the Spiritual Exercises.* Edited and translated by Philip Endean and Joseph A. Munitiz. London: Penguin Books, 1996.

Jerome, St. Epistle 22: To Eustochium.

————. Epistle 130: To Demetrias.

John Paul II, Pope. *Roman Triptych: Meditations.* Translated by Jerzy Peterkiewicz. Vatican: Libreria Editrice Vaticana, 2003.

Jones, Pamela M. *Altarpieces and Their Viewers in the Churches of Rome from Caravaggio to Guido Reni.* Visual Culture in Early Modernity. Aldershot, England: Ashgate, 2008.

Kempis, Thomas à. *The Imitation of Christ.* Milwaukee: Bruce, 1940.

Langdon, Helen. *Caravaggio: A Life.* London: Pimlico, 1999.

Lev, Elizabeth. "A Marian Interpretation of Michelangelo's Roman *Pietà.*" In *Revisioning: Critical Methods of Seeing Christianity in the History of Art*, edited by James Romaine and Linda Stratford, 207–224. Eugene, OR: Cascade Books, 2013.

Luther, Martin. "Auslegung Des Ersten Buches Mose." In *Dr. Martin Luthers Sämtliche Schriften*. Edited by Johann Georg Walch. St. Louis: Concordia Publishing House, 1880–1910.

————. *The Complete Sermons of Martin Luther.* Vol. 7, Grand Rapids, MI: Baker Books, 2000.

————. "Let Your Sins Be Strong: A Letter from Luther to Melanchthon, Letter No. 99." In *The Wartburg (Segment) from Dr. Martin Luthers Saemmtliche Schriften*. St. Louis: Concordia Publishing House, 1521.

————. *Luther's Works on CD-ROM.* Philadelphia: Fortress Press, 2001.

————. *Martin Luther's 95 Theses: With the Pertinent Documents from the History of the Reformation.* Edited by Kurt Aland. Saint Louis: Concordia Publishing House, 1967.

————. "On the Babylonish Captivity of the Church." Christian Classics Ethereal Library, https://www.ccel.org/ccel/luther/first_prin.v.iii.html.

Bibliography

———. *The Table Talk of Martin Luther*. London: George Bell, 1902.

Magnuson, Torgil. *Rome in the Age of Bernini*. 2 vols. Kungl Vitterhets, Historie Och Antikvitets Akademiens Handlingar Antikvariska Serien. Stockholm, Sweden: Almqvist and Wiksell International, 1986.

Natali, Antonio. "Andrea Del Sarto, a Model of Thought and Language." In *The Cinquecento in Florence: "Modern Manner" and Counter-Reformation*. Edited by Carlo Falciani and Antonio Natali, 2739. Firenze: Mandragora, 2017.

Newman, John Henry. *The Second Eve*. Charlotte, NC: Tan Books, 1991.

Ostrow, Steven F. *Art and Spirituality in Counter-Reformation Rome: The Sistine and Pauline Chapels in S. Maria Maggiore*. Monuments of Papal Rome. Cambridge: Cambridge University Press, 1996.

———. "Counter-Reformation and the End of the Century." In *Artistic Centers of the Italian Renaissance: Rome*, edited by Marcia Hall, 246–259. New York: Cambridge University Press, 2005.

Paleotti, Gabriele. *Discourse on Sacred and Profane Images*. Edited by Paolo Prodi. Translated by William McCuaig. Los Angeles, CA: Getty Research Institute, 2012.

Paul III, Pope. Encyclical *Sublimis Dei* (May 29, 1537). http://www.papalencyclicals.net/paul03/p3subli.htm.

Price, David. *Albrecht Dürer's Renaissance: Humanism, Reformation, and the Art of Faith*. Studies in Medieval and Early Modern Civilization. Ann Arbor: University of Michigan Press, 2003.

Prodi, Paolo. *Il Cardinale Gabriele Paleotti (1522–1597)*. 2 vols. Uomini e Dottrine. Roma: Edizioni di storia e letteratura, 1959.

Reid, Stanford W. "Bernard of Clairvaux in the Thought of John Calvin." *Westminster Theological Journal* 41, no. 1 (1978).

Sebregondi, Ludovica. "Churches, Convents, Monasteries and Confraternities in Counter Reformation Florence." In *The Cinquecento in Florence: "Modern Manner" and Counter-Reformation*, edited by Carlo Falciani and Antonio Natali, 107–117. Firenze: Mandragora, 2017.

Shakespeare, William. *The Norton William Shakespeare*. 2nd ed. Edited by Stephen Greenblatt, Walter Cohen, Jean E. Howard, and Katharine Eisaman Maus. London: W. W. Norton, 2008.

Shea, William R., and Mariano Artigas. *Galileo in Rome: The Rise and Fall of a Troublesome Genius*. Oxford: Oxford University Press, 2003.

Stark, Rodney. "The Misfortune of State Churches, Forced Piety and Bigotry." In *Reformation Myths: Five Centuries of Misconceptions and (Some) Misfortunes*. London: Society for Promoting Christian Knowledge, 2017.

Sullivan, Cornelius. "Pope Francis and Caravaggio." *Italian Insider*, September 25, 2013. http://www.italianinsider.it/?q=node/1694.

Teresa of Avila, St. *The Life of St. Teresa of Jesus, of the Order of Our Lady of Carmel*. Translated by David Lewis. 3rd ed. London: T. Baker, 1904.

Tertullian. *Apologeticum*. Tertullian Project, http://www.tertullian.org/works/apologeticum.htm.

Trent, Council of. *Canons and Decrees of the Council of Trent*. Rockford, IL: TAN Books, 1978.

Turner, Nicholas. *Federico Barocci*. Paris: Société Nouvelle Adam Biro, 2000.

Varriano, John L. *Caravaggio: The Art of Realism*. University Park, PA: Pennsylvania State University Press, 2006.

Vasari, Giorgio. *The Lives of the Artists*. London: Penguin Books, 1965.

Weiber, Walther. "The Representation of Ecstasy." In *Bernini in Perspective*, edited by George C. Bauer, 75–89. Englewood Cliffs, NJ: Prentice-Hall, 1976.

Sophia Institute

Sophia Institute is a nonprofit institution that seeks to nurture the spiritual, moral, and cultural life of souls and to spread the Gospel of Christ in conformity with the authentic teachings of the Roman Catholic Church.

Sophia Institute Press fulfills this mission by offering translations, reprints, and new publications that afford readers a rich source of the enduring wisdom of mankind.

Sophia Institute also operates two popular online Catholic resources: CrisisMagazine.com and CatholicExchange.com.

Crisis Magazine provides insightful cultural analysis that arms readers with the arguments necessary for navigating the ideological and theological minefields of the day. *Catholic Exchange* provides world news from a Catholic perspective as well as daily devotionals and articles that will help you to grow in holiness and live a life consistent with the teachings of the Church.

In 2013, Sophia Institute launched Sophia Institute for Teachers to renew and rebuild Catholic culture through service to Catholic education. With the goal of nurturing the spiritual, moral, and cultural life of souls, and an abiding respect for the role and work of teachers, we strive to provide materials and programs that are at once enlightening to the mind and ennobling to the heart; faithful and complete, as well as useful and practical.

Sophia Institute gratefully recognizes the Solidarity Association for preserving and encouraging the growth of our apostolate over the course of many years. Without their generous and timely support, this book would not be in your hands.

www.SophiaInstitute.com
www.CatholicExchange.com
www.CrisisMagazine.com
www.SophiaInstituteforTeachers.org

Sophia Institute Press® is a registered trademark of Sophia Institute.
Sophia Institute is a tax-exempt institution as defined by the
Internal Revenue Code, Section 501(c)(3). Tax I.D. 22-2548708.